LET ME BE FRANK WITH YOU

A CANDID GUIDE TO CORPORATE LIFE LESSONS

FRANK LAZARO

CONTENTS

Let Me be Frank with You: A candid guide to corporate life lessons

Frank Lazaro LLC

www.franklazaro.com

Publishing services provided by Believers Book Services

Cover design: Terry Dugan

Cover image by Birti Ishar on Unsplash

Editing: Marcus Costantino

Interior layout: Justin Shreeves & Ben Wolf

ISBN-13: 979-8-9887789-0-5

ePub ISBN: 979-8-9887789-1-2

PDF ISBN: 979-8-9887789-2-9

First Printing, 2023

Printed in The United States of America

ACKNOWLEDGMENTS

First, I want to acknowledge and express gratitude to all the people I have worked with. Some have taught me how to be better and focus on what is important to achieve my goals—mentors, coaches, peers, and alike. Others have taught me exactly what not to do—some were just terrible people, while others were outputs of their environments. Both sets of people have taught me a lot. It just depends on whether it was good or whether it was bad.

There have been a good number of individuals who have played a significant role in my personal life, which naturally bled over to influence my professional life. In some cases, professional relationships turned into lifelong personal friendships. From Jamie who convinced me to head out to Cingular Wireless while we were in grad school to Tom at Deloitte who helped me develop thick skin to deal with difficult people. All had an impact. There are more people than I expected when I started writing this section.

I look back and think, "Nah! There aren't that many," until I started writing. Whether it was emotional support, inspiration, or advice, I know I will forget some names. I tried to do a stream of typing and the names that came out first and in no particular order included Evan, Hayden, Susan, Doug, Kelly, Jamie, Tom, Joe (and there are two of them), Tony, Stephen, Katja, Max, Bianca, and probably a few others. I won't mention the names that have a negative spin to them, but that list is a lot longer. But I do thank those folks in the latter category: You helped write this book in a lot of ways.

I wanted to express my appreciation for those who contributed both directly and indirectly to this book. Our interactions, the projects we worked on, and the companies we worked for helped frame these chapters. The chaos and the silliness we experienced together almost wrote this book without my help.

The inspiration for this book started almost 10 years ago when I started to just take notes — some would call it journaling. I don't journal, or do I? So, I started out to capture the crazy that occurs at work (and no matter what job I was doing or company I was at, there was always something crazy happening). Once I started to see themes, the chapters started to build themselves. And over time, I added more detail and context. 10,000 words, then it would sit for a while, and I wouldn't touch it or write anything for a long time. I'd get an itch and focus on trying to finish a chapter or two. This went on for years, with some years producing more writing than others.

In the last year or so, I have been inspired to finally finish this dang book. Personally, I started the journey of losing weight, getting in shape, and eating better. I had new people enter my life who not only inspired me but affirmed me and encouraged me in ways that hadn't happened in years. Finally, I found some footing through speaking at conferences, teaching, coaching, and mentoring more. My creative juices were flowing.

I can't forget to thank ChatGPT. Artificial intelligence has helped a lot in filling in the gaps. It helped with idea starters and concepts that allowed me to round out the rest of this book. I have always loved technology and think the best is yet to come when it comes to AI.

This book has been more than ten years in the making. I never thought I would get around to finishing it. I am thankful for those around me and feel blessed by those who are close to me. I am usually full of crazy ideas—like who wants to start a photography non-profit!?

PREFACE

This book is full of contradictions. In the unlikely event you are in a situation where I said something in this book contradicts other parts of this book, and you are unsure what to do, then you are probably screwed. I can't help you. No book or advice is going to help. Ok, maybe not screwed, but you'll have to make it up as you go along. Your gut instinct will get you mostly there. Just trust your gut. Or maybe you are screwed. You will eventually find out which. Anyway. Common sense helps a lot too. All too often, many people sacrifice common sense, which would most likely help them 80-90% of the time.

But this book is full of my real-world examples, and the names have been changed to protect the stupid and the impacted. Most people aren't innocent, and it is okay to blame them because they are probably blaming you behind your back to your co-workers or your manager or both. Not trying to be negative, just being truthful. There are some good people you will work with and a lot of terrible people who are self-centered and are in it for themselves. They will do anything, including throwing you under a bus, to get ahead. Just as with driving a vehicle, always be on the defense. Just be a good person and do the right thing, right up to the point at which you can't or don't need to. As the old saying goes, everyone wants to be a gangster until it is time to be a gangster. There are three kinds of people: Sheep, wolves, and sheepdogs. Be the last one. Nice and playful right up until the wolves show up.

It is also full of common sense, at least to me. There are plenty of facepalm moments, and there will be countless times when you say, "Well, no kidding." But, as they say, common sense is not common.

Some of these stories are like videos that show "conference calls in real life." While funny, we all know how sad these things are IRL (in real life), as the young kids say—I think.

I digress. Ultimately, when I thought about authoring this book, I thought about picking a topic, just one or two related topics, and espousing my knowledge on you or vomiting it out just like every other business and self-help book. Blah, blah, blah. You are better. Nope. You probably suck at what you do and have no real desire to get better. This may or may not be your fault, but there is a way out. There is a way to get better.

As I started writing, I couldn't help thinking about all the crazy, funny, and stupid stuff that happens in the corporate world that most take as normal. Then we go to a conference or offsite or training and come back with all the knowledge to fix everything. But when the rubber meets the road, we all fall back into the habits that allow us to survive but never to grow and learn. Well, maybe the only thing you learn is the ability to survive.

At some point, you want to do more than survive. You want to grow professionally. I ran face-first into several walls and lost my compass. I felt aimless and lacked direction in my career. Some of this had to do with my stubbornness, my belief that I knew better or was smarter than my current situation. But once I was able to clear my head, take my head out of my own and focus on how I could grow, things improved.

It doesn't all happen at once or overnight. It takes time. It takes self-awareness. It takes admitting, "I need to be better." It takes more trying and less complaining.

People tend to avoid having honest conversations. The fear of offending someone or hurting their feelings overpowers you, and you soften what you would have said. This is to the detriment of not only the receiver but also of you.

In addition to not having honest conversations with others, the one person you should always be completely honest with is yourself, and to be honest, you are not. You lie to yourself all the time.

In the book *Unfu*k Yourself* by Gary John Bishop, he says the one person you talk to the most is yourself. You have the uncanny ability to talk yourself out of or into anything. The basic element of this is that you need to get out of your head and move into action.

Honestly, it is not easy. But you need to get moving to make any changes.

If I said to you, get better at your job or be more confident, you are not likely to just magically be better at your job, nor would you become confident or have confidence. So to get better, you have to change your mindset. Think differently about your abilities and have an honest conversation with yourself about how you can improve things.

One of my goals with this book is to show you, through stories, how to be a better person— to suck less. I find that stories are the best way to get your point across. Plus, the receiver can then relate to it and know others have gone through or experienced the same things. And if we are being honest, nothing you experience is unique. It has happened to someone, somewhere before. You are not special. You are not unique. Most likely, you are a dumbass.

As Gary John Bishop states in his book, *UnFu*k Yourself*, you are achieving exactly what you set your mind to, nothing more, nothing less. If you want to achieve more, go achieve it. Want to be better? Go make yourself better. What is stopping you?

Throughout this book, I hit on topics that are important to me, important to how I see where I have failed and where others did not live up to my expectations. There is always a lesson and a teachable moment in everything we experience, especially in a work environment. You are always going to work with or collaborate with someone you can't stand, someone who always does the wrong thing, says the wrong thing, or derails a project. There will always be someone who doesn't pull their weight but takes credit. You'll come across people who just want to see the world burn, figuratively—maybe literally. But if the latter is the case, call HR.

You'll also work with people you love, someone who makes work bearable, someone who makes work and projects go, and someone you can trust. You will also work with people you like who aren't worth a wet blanket and don't do anything. The question is this: Do you confront them? No need to answer; I already know you don't. You make excuses for the people you like and bad mouth the ones you don't. You are not alone; everyone does it. Again, you are not unique or special.

The corporate world can be a chaotic place. It's filled with people who are either trying to make a name for themselves or trying to keep their heads above water. In such an environment, it's easy to lose sight of what's important and get caught up in the drama. This book aims to provide you with some guidance on how to navigate this world and thrive in it.

In the chapter on emotional intelligence is the ability to understand and manage your emotions and those of others. It's an essential skill in the workplace, as it allows you to work effectively with people from different backgrounds and personalities. Emotional intelligence can also help you avoid misunderstandings and conflicts.

One way to develop emotional intelligence is to practice active listening. Active listening means paying attention to what the other person is saying and acknowledging their feelings. This can help you build rapport with others and create a positive work environment.

Another way to develop emotional intelligence is to practice empathy. Empathy means putting yourself in someone else's shoes and trying to understand their perspective. This can help you communicate more effectively and resolve conflicts more quickly.

There is also a chapter on being an office prepper, which means being prepared for anything that might come your way. It means having a plan for when things go wrong and being ready to handle emergencies. This could mean having backup plans for important projects or keeping emergency supplies at your desk.

One way to be an office prepper is to develop contingency plans for important projects. This means identifying potential risks and developing a plan to mitigate them. It's also important to communicate these plans to your team so that everyone is on the same page.

Another way to be an office prepper is to keep a well-stocked emergency kit at your desk. This could include things like first aid supplies, a flashlight, and non-perishable snacks. Being prepared for emergencies can help you stay calm and focused when things get hectic.

We can't write a business book unless we have a chapter on teamwork—the good and bad. Teamwork is the ability to work effectively with others towards a common goal. It's essential in the workplace, as it allows you to achieve more than you could on your own. Good teamwork requires clear communication, trust, and mutual respect.

One way to improve teamwork is to establish clear goals and expectations. This means defining what success looks like and what each team member's role is. It's also important to communicate these goals and expectations to everyone on the team.

Another way to improve teamwork is to encourage open communication. This means creating a safe space for team members to share their ideas and concerns. It's also important to actively listen to others and consider their perspectives.

Business books tend to shy away from how to deal with criticism, and when I say "deal with," I mean how to truly handle it. Criticism is an inevitable part of the workplace. It can be difficult to hear, but it's important to learn how to handle it effectively. One way to do this is to focus on the feedback itself rather than the person delivering it. This means separating the message from the messenger and trying to understand the feedback objectively.

Another way to handle criticism is to practice active listening. This means giving the person delivering the feedback your full attention and acknowledging their perspective. It's also important to ask clarifying questions and seek to understand their reasoning.

A chapter on focusing is important. I know I struggle with it at times. Focusing means being able to concentrate on one task at a time and avoid distractions. It's an essential skill in the workplace, as it allows you to be more productive and efficient. One way to improve focus is to eliminate distractions. This could mean turning off your phone or email notifications or working in a quiet space.

Another way to improve focus is to break large tasks into smaller ones. This can make the task more manageable and help you avoid feeling overwhelmed. It's also important to prioritize tasks based on their importance and urgency.

People are terrible at networking, so I added a chapter on that as well. Business networking means building relationships with people in your industry or related fields to advance your career or business. It's an essential part of professional development, as it allows you to expand your network and learn from others. One way to improve your networking skills is to attend industry events and conferences. This allows you to meet new people and learn about the latest trends and developments in your field.

Another way to improve your networking skills is to be proactive in reaching out to people. This could mean sending a LinkedIn message or email to someone you admire or respect in your field. It's important to be genuine and specific in your communication and to offer something of value in return.

Who does not love office politics? Of course, I would add a chapter on it. Office politics refers to the complex power dynamics and relationships within a workplace. It's important to navigate office politics effectively to advance your career and achieve your goals. One way to do this is to build alliances with people who share your goals and values.

This means identifying people who can support you and help you achieve your objectives.

Another way to navigate office politics is to avoid getting involved in gossip or drama. This means staying neutral and not taking sides in conflicts or disagreements. It's also important to maintain a professional demeanor and avoid letting emotions get the better of you.

Trust plays a big part throughout this book, so there is a chapter on trust. We all know trust is essential in the workplace, as it allows you to work effectively with others and achieve common goals. Building trust requires consistent communication, honesty, and transparency. One way to build trust is to follow through on your commitments. This means doing what you say you will do and delivering on your promises.

Another way to build trust is to admit your mistakes and take responsibility for your actions. This shows that you are accountable and willing to learn from your mistakes. It's also important to communicate openly and honestly with your colleagues and superiors.

Navigating the corporate world can be challenging, but it's also full of opportunities for growth and development. By practicing emotional intelligence, being an office prepper, working effectively in teams, handling criticism, focusing on your goals, networking, navigating office politics, and building trust, you can thrive in this environment and achieve your professional goals. Remember, it's not about being perfect but about being willing to learn and grow from your experiences.

With all this setup, let's jump into it. I hope you enjoy it, or if you don't, I probably already have your money for the book, so all is good.

EMOTIONAL INTELLIGENCE

It all starts with being emotionally aware, emotionally aware of yourself, and emotionally aware of others. Someone's body language and other non-verbal clues. When you are talking with someone, do you pay attention to what they are saying, or do you watch their body language? Are you listening to respond or listening to understand? Someone's body language holds more insight into that person than what they are saying. Is the person nervous? Are they sweating, or is their voice dry? The clues are everywhere. This then begs the question, how are you using this knowledge and awareness to your advantage?

I find making someone less nervous builds trust. Acknowledging them in a way that is not threatening helps them realize you are there to help.

Truly listening to what people are saying (rather than listening to respond to what they are saying) is the most important thing you can do to become emotionally aware. Understanding why someone is telling you something will help you respond or not respond. I have repeatedly observed that people think they must respond when the option of not responding is wholly proper at times. The power of not responding or reacting is enormous. It is worthwhile to note that people sometimes say things and do things just to get a reaction. They do things and say things to feel power over you. They know it will upset you or get under your skin. So, listening to what they are saying and why they are saying it gives you power and not them.

Read people, read the room. Understand your audience. People tend to be so self-absorbed that they do not invest in what is around them. They are so focused on responding to what someone is saying because they want to be heard or they want to make a point—thinking they are "winning" when they have lost. They just do not know they've lost. This is a systematic failure of most people, and sadly most do not realize they are doing it.

To be honest, I was like this in my early career. I would be impatient. I would not listen and struggled to always be heard or try to make my point. Just like a little kid waving his hand wildly to get someone's attention, and when it was my turn, I would just blurt out something not relevant. Basically, I was telling everyone I barely belonged in the room. I was not a leader. I was barely a contributor and made myself look foolish. The crazy part is that I did not know it. I was too busy worrying about getting my voice heard that I did not listen. I was not perceptive enough to understand the room, or the people around me.

It has little to do with being heard and more to do with listening, understanding, and then being heard. Have you ever been in a meeting and heard someone talk, and you ask yourself, what is this person talking about? Well, someone has said that about you.

Ask yourself these questions. What is the point of what I am saying? Am I adding any value to moving this conversation along to a meaningful conclusion? If you do not have answers to those questions, shut up. Listen. Absorb. Then contribute or don't. Too many times, people just think they need to say something for fear of being labeled as not taking part. There are no participation trophies, just career-limiting behavior. Sometimes, just not responding and listening will help get the conversation moving in the direction of a solution.

How many times have you felt you have had the same meeting over and over? Y have meetings on the same topic and never get to a resolution, only to meet again about the same topic. Some of these meetings seem to grow over time too. A meeting that starts with four key stakeholders expands to include six in the next meeting, then ten in the next. It is like a fungus, growing and growing over time.

I think some people just like to live in this kind of swirl —people who just like to live in a constant state of distress and want to drag as many people into the ditch as humanly possible.

I recall sitting in meetings to discuss our next marketing promotion. In what should have been an ongoing meeting with a few people, it always ended up including more people than required or needed. There were a lot of opinions and discussions with people who really didn't have a say but were in the meeting anyway. Not sure why. After listening to what a lot of attendees were saying and how the meeting progressed, we could never come to a solution at any of these meetings.

Thinking about how I could be more effective and move these meetings along, I decided to have a separate meeting with just one key stakeholder before the bigger meeting. Knowing that I couldn't kill the bigger meeting for the endless butthurt that would quickly consume my time, and after spending a good amount of listening, I felt this was the right course of action.

With the separate pre-meeting, most of the decisions were made, and discussion and debate were limited because the meeting went from asking people's opinions to telling them what we were doing. I was able to blunt any questions with the preparation I completed beforehand. Again, listening to what people were saying and what they were most likely to complain about, I was able to ready my answers and retorts beforehand. Allowing me to dismiss them and move on quickly.

I did not need promotional input in customer service. Sorry, just didn't. Not unless the promotion I was sending increased call volume or was confusing to the customer (which would increase service calls) was their opinion needed. You run customer service; I run marketing. Stay in your lane and quit messing up my meeting.

I was able to find a solution to my problem by listening to what was being said instead of diving deep into crap and fighting with people in the meeting.

Using emotional awareness and active listening, you can find solutions to the problems your co-workers create. They are listening to respond. They are listening just long enough to be able to speak. They are not listening to understand.

An important aspect of this is having high emotional intelligence. Be able to read a room or a person and effectively communicate with that person. Do not personalize or become emotional: just listen and hear what is being said. Then communicate back effectively. Adjust your communication styles to the audience, even if that is an audience of one.

Bruce Lee once said, "I'm not in this world to live up to

your expectations, and you are not in this world to live up to mine. You are you, I am I. And if by chance we find each other, it's beautiful." Embrace emotional intelligence to improve emotional awareness and emotional regulation. Do not be over-emotional; just understand yourself and others better so that you can work together towards a solution. The problems people will present can be solved faster if they know that you are listening to them with empathy instead of trying to solve the problem for them.

"But what about meetings?" I hear some of you asking. Well, how many meetings have been derailed because someone thinks their opinion is more important or has a habit of venting? How many pointless meetings have been had because someone feels they need to be heard? Have you ever sat down and said, "Hey, what do you want to talk about?" and then actually listen? No butthurt or emotional responses. Just emotional awareness will improve emotional regulation (and vice versa), which leads to emotional intelligence during these meetings, which leads to progress.

Bottom line: Listen actively and communicate effectively for better results.

Emotional awareness throughout the day can make things much more effective. You are not always at work; however, your emotional self is always there (no matter where). Using emotional awareness deliberately will increase regulation which increases emotional intelligence making everything better. At the least, emotional self-awareness is beneficial to emotional regulation, which will help you during emotional situations at work.

Emotional awareness and emotional regulation are important for emotional intelligence, which can improve how you deal with problems both on your own and in groups. Using emotional awareness deliberately improves emotional regulation, which increases emotional intelligence. Emotional awareness throughout the day also helps us regulate our emotions better. By recognizing what is happening to us emotionally, we can make adjustments that might be needed to prevent an overreaction or under-response where it would not have been detected otherwise. The benefits of this are improved relationships at work, better decision-making, lower stress levels, the ability to handle difficult conversations more productively, and increased motivation & drive for success.

What emotional intelligence cannot help you with is the ability to read people's thoughts. It can't tell you what other people are feeling, but it can give you the tools to deal with them more effectively when you have accurate emotional information.

Sometimes emotional responses are hard to regulate because we may not always know why we feel a certain way about something or someone. Emotional awareness through emotional self-awareness helps us become aware of our emotional state, which allows us to better self-regulate our emotional response. Sometimes this requires some emotional processing to determine what has triggered that emotional response and how best to handle it moving forward.

For example, if somebody walks into your office visibly upset, even though they are smiling at you, there is likely to be some emotional self-awareness to allow you to either respond accordingly or remain calm. Combined with emotional regulation, emotional awareness can make all the difference in how you deal with emotional situations at work.

Emotional intelligence is the ability to both understand

emotions and what drives our behavior, as well as manage our emotional responses to different circumstances. Emotional awareness is one of the key components of emotional intelligence, which allows us to know what we are feeling and then use this knowledge to help regulate our emotions. Being emotionally aware will benefit your career in many ways, including allowing you to better understand others' emotional states so that you can help them out when needed. Self-awareness is also important for emotional regulation, which helps you avoid overreacting or under-responding in emotional situations.

Emotional awareness is a crucial skill for emotional intelligence, which improves emotional regulation and positive coping strategies when times get tough. Knowing your emotional state allows you to make adjustments that might be needed to prevent an overreaction or under-response. The benefits of emotional awareness include improved relationships at work, better decision-making, lower stress levels, the ability to handle difficult conversations more productively, and increased motivation & drive for success. Emotional self-awareness is a key component of emotional intelligence. Overall, emotional awareness throughout the day not only helps us regulate our emotions better but also ensures we are acting from a place of emotional insight rather than without any understanding of our emotional state. Being aware of how others feel can allow us to react accordingly, which helps us avoid emotional mistakes that could have been made otherwise.

Emotional awareness throughout the day not only helps us regulate our emotions better but also ensures we are acting from a place of emotional insight rather than without any understanding of our emotional state. Being aware of how others feel can allow us to react accordingly, which helps us avoid emotional mistakes that could have been made otherwise. Emotionally sensitive people tend to be more useful in emotional situations at work where being able to read others' emotional states is helpful, especially when you might need help staying composed or managing your own emotions.

Understanding EQ or having emotional intelligence can make you an effective leader and a successful person. EQ is defined by the Oxford dictionary as "the capacity to be aware of, control, and express one's emotions, and to handle interpersonal relationships judiciously and empathetically." EQ essentially means having emotional intelligence, but EQ can be broken down into two parts: EQ-I, which is the ability to identify and assess your own emotions; EQ-o, which is the ability to identify those of others.

The foundation for an EQ lies in self-awareness and self-management. Self-awareness is understanding who you are at a core level—your values, beliefs, personality traits, and limits—so that you can strengthen empowering connections with other people while avoiding connections that push against your limits or needs. Being able to manage yourself means having the EQ skills to stay clear and level-headed even in emotionally charged situations.

If you manage your EQ, you can strengthen relation-ships with others while setting up healthy emotional boundaries that are mutually beneficial to everyone involved. EQ helps create good habits of mind that let you turn potentially negative situations into opportunities for learning and growth.

For example, EQ allowed the early American president Abraham Lincoln to empathize with his Confederate prede-cessor Jefferson Davis. Although their political views were diametrically opposed, Lincoln was able to put himself in

Davis's shoes and have some respect for his challenges without being ambivalent about the war. In doing so, he was able to maintain a more civil tone in their correspondence. EQ allowed him to understand his counterpart's experience while staying firm on his position.

In another example, EQ enabled Jill Kelley, a Florida socialite and one of the women who exposed Gen. David Petraeus' affair, to handle her emotional crisis without alienating her connections with others or creating a situation that would harm herself or others. After receiving threatening messages from the other woman involved in the scandal, Kelley had no qualms about going straight to top officials at military intelligence agencies—including Petraeus himself—to share what she knew and seek advice on how best to proceed.

It takes EQ skills for people to be able to communicate with others without having to raise their voices, be passive-aggressive, or lash out in anger. EQ allows people to handle difficult conversations with an air of flexibility that keeps everyone's best interests at heart.

Being able to express your emotions also means being able to understand and manage others' emotions. EQ lets you properly express empathy toward another person without trying too hard (which would read insincere) or not enough (which would come across as cold). For example, after receiving her son's diagnosis of autism spectrum disorder, reality star Kim Kardashian took some time off from the public spotlight before opening up about what she had gone through for the benefit of parents who were facing the same issue. Her ability to recognize her own needs while expressing them allowed her to respect those of other parents.

People with EQ can manage their emotions and stay

calm in even the most emotionally charged situations. EQ also allows you to step outside of your perspective and see things from another's point of view, which is one of the defining features of emotional intelligence. EQ helps people think not just about their feelings but those of others as well. EQ sets the tone for relationships by creating a sense that everyone involved cares about each other and wants what's best for everyone else at heart—a sentiment that only gets stronger when people practice EQ daily.

Being a good leader requires a high EQ and using it effectively and appropriately. EQ is what allows you to empathize with your employees, understand their problems and challenges, and motivate them toward achieving the goals of the organization. EQ helps leaders build trust within teams while making it clear where each team member fits in so that everyone understands their roles and feels fulfilled by the work they do. EQ helps managers see what's working well among employees and how to let those successes grow further rather than taking credit for them themselves. EQ helps managers identify and solve issues before they become major problems or conflicts that can tear a team apart. EQ lets leaders push forward without becoming pushy, which reduces stress on the entire company—and its people—allowing progress to happen smoothly instead of through force.

EQ is what makes leaders inspirational.

A high EQ can help improve an entire organization's performance, opening doors for others to succeed while helping the company work toward its long-term goals. EQ can bring out people's best qualities and lead them to commit more wholeheartedly to the company mission, which in turn leads companies to reach new levels of greatness. EQ allows employees who might otherwise be introverted or quiet to express themselves clearly and confidently—creating better relationships with co-workers and supervisors alike—which benefits everyone in a big way. EQ helps leaders recognize when it's time to make changes in their department—and even in the company as a whole—so that they can adjust direction when needed without worrying about resistance from other members of the organization. EQ helps leaders build consensus among colleagues through open dialogue that keeps the focus on the topic at hand instead of devolving into petty arguments.

EQ also affects people's lives outside work, though it manifests itself in different ways. EQ makes it possible for people to relate to others in strong, real ways. EQ gives people the ability not just to bond with others but also to collaborate and compromise so that everyone gets a say and feels satisfied by the result whether it's an improved relationship or a finished product. EQ helps you connect with family and friends while staying true and confident around them—and without letting their feelings affect you too deeply when conflicts do come up. EQ is what allows parents not only to get along with their children but to do so while maintaining the authority needed to keep everyone safe and raised responsibly. EQ is what helps people cultivate relationships with their children by treating them like unique individuals who deserve respect, empathy, laughter, and love. EQ makes it possible for children to look forward to spending time with their parents—especially when they know that there won't be any fights or arguments at home—so that they can grow up in a positive environment instead of a toxic or emotionally draining one.

With emotional intelligence, you can achieve emotional freedom from your emotions. EQ allows people to identify, assess, and control both negative and positive feelings inside themselves, which provides them with a sense of well-being that comes from knowing that their feelings aren't getting in the way.

When it comes to work decisions, it's essential to be able to separate your emotions from the decision-making process. This doesn't mean that you should ignore your emotions altogether, but rather that you should be aware of them and take them into account without letting them control your decision-making.

There are a few ways to do this. First, it's important to be aware of your own emotional triggers. What are the things that tend to set off your emotions? Once you know what these are, you can try to avoid them or at least be prepared for them.

Second, when you're feeling emotional, take a step back and try to assess the situation dispassionately. What are the facts of the situation? What are the options? What are the risks and rewards of each option? Once you've looked at the situation objectively, you'll be able to make a more informed decision.

Third, don't let your emotions cloud your judgment. If you're feeling angry, for example, you might be tempted to lash out or make a rash decision. But if you can take a deep breath and count to 10, you'll give yourself time to calm down and think more clearly.

Finally, remember that it's okay to have emotions. They're normal and healthy. But if they're preventing you from making effective decisions, it's time to take steps to gain emotional freedom. With emotional intelligence, you can learn how to separate your emotions from your work decisions and make the best choices for both your career and your well-being.

There are plenty of books on emotional intelligence or

EQ. There are plenty of blogs, internet posts, and podcasts that address this topic. A common and popular one is *Emotional Intelligence 2.0* by Travis Bradberry. While all of these are good, they are not a substitute for general self-awareness. If you want to improve your emotional intelligence, read about it, listen to podcasts about it, but most importantly—practice it. One of the best ways to do this is to become self-aware.

When you have an emotion, stop and think about it. Don't try to bottle it up or push it away. Emotions are just energy, and they are meant to be released. However, we don't always want to release our emotions in an uncontrolled way. That's where awareness comes in. Further, don't let people know how you feel because they might try to use it against you. Be in control.

Awareness allows us to see our emotions for what they are— energy that is meant to be released. It also allows us to control the release of that energy. So, when you're feeling an emotion, take a few deep breaths and allow yourself to feel it. Don't try to push it away. Once you've acknowledged it, you can release it in a way that is helpful, not harmful.

One of the most important things to remember about emotional intelligence is that it's not about being perfect. We all have emotions, and we all must deal with them. The goal is to be aware of them and to manage them in a way that is healthy and helpful. With practice, you can learn how to do this. And when you do, you'll find that your work decisions are much easier and more effective than they ever were before.

Emotional intelligence (EQ) is the capacity to be aware of and manage one's own emotions and the emotions of others. It is a critical skill for anyone in the workforce. After all, our emotions play a big role in how we interact with others, how we make decisions, and how we deal with stress.

If you want to be successful in your career, it's essential that you learn how to separate your emotions from your work decisions. This doesn't mean that you should ignore your emotions altogether; rather, you should be aware of them and take them into account without letting them control your decision-making.

There are a few ways to do this. First, it's important to be aware of your emotional triggers. What are the things that tend to set off your emotions? Once you know what these are, you can be more mindful of them and take steps to avoid or diffuse them.

Second, it's helpful to approach work decisions objectively. What are the facts of the situation? What are the options? What are the risks and rewards of each option? Once you've looked at the situation objectively, you'll be able to make a more informed reaction. Remember, you are the one in control, and you need to be able to manage your emotions and, as importantly, recognize others' emotions. This way, you will be able to formulate the best result.

2

WHEN AND WHEN NOT TO POKE A BEAR

The phrase "poking a bear" is a metaphor used to describe the act of intentionally provoking someone who is known to have a strong or volatile personality or temperament. It's a risky behavior that can have unintended and sometimes harmful consequences.

In the animal world, bears are known for their strength, aggression, and ability to cause harm. In the same way, "poking a bear" is an action that is likely to trigger a strong emotional response from the person being provoked.

For example, if someone is known to have a short temper and a tendency to lash out when angry, intentionally doing something to provoke them would be considered "poking the bear." This could take the form of teasing, insulting, or otherwise agitating the person in question.

In other situations, "poking the bear" might refer to a reckless or foolish act that is likely to have negative consequences. For instance, if someone is known to be particularly sensitive about a certain topic, bringing it up in conversation to upset them would be considered "poking the bear."

In general, the phrase "poking the bear" is used to caution against intentionally provoking someone who is known to be volatile or easily angered. Doing so can lead to conflict, damage relationships, and create unnecessary tension.

In a professional setting or workplace, "poking the bear" can take on many different forms. It could be as simple as making a sarcastic comment to a colleague who is already feeling stressed or as serious as undermining a coworker's work or authority.

Some examples of "poking the bear" in a professional setting might include the following:

- **Criticizing a coworker's work in public**: This can be particularly damaging if the criticism is unwarranted or delivered in a confrontational way. It can create a hostile work environment and damage trust among team members.
- **Ignoring someone's boundaries or requests**: If a colleague has asked to be left alone or has set clear boundaries around their time or workload, ignoring these requests can make the person feel disrespected or undervalued.
- **Making insensitive comments or jokes**: If someone is known to be sensitive about a certain topic, making jokes or comments about it can create a hostile work environment and make it difficult for the person to feel comfortable or respected at work.
- **Questioning someone's authority or expertise**: If a coworker is in a position of authority or has

expertise in a particular area, questioning their decisions or knowledge can create tension and make it difficult for the team to work together effectively.

IN GENERAL, "POKING THE BEAR" in a professional setting is a risky behavior that can have serious consequences. It's important to be aware of your coworkers' boundaries and sensitivities and to always communicate respectfully and professionally.

Dealing with "poking the bear" behavior in a professional setting can be challenging, but there are several strategies you can use to mitigate its impact and prevent it from escalating.

Here are some recommendations on how to deal with this type of behavior when you see it or are on the receiving end of it:

- **Stay calm and avoid reacting emotionally**: Try to stay calm and avoid reacting emotionally. Responding in kind or escalating the situation will only make things worse.
- **Set boundaries**: It may be necessary to set clear boundaries and communicate them firmly but respectfully. Let the person know that their behavior is not acceptable and that you expect to be treated with respect.
- **Document the behavior**: If the behavior is persistent or has serious consequences, it may be necessary to document the behavior and report it

to a supervisor or an HR representative. Keep a record of any incidents, including dates, times, and details of what happened.

- **Seek support from colleagues or a supervisor**: If you're feeling overwhelmed or unsure of how to handle the situation, seek support from colleagues or a supervisor. They may be able to provide advice, mediation, or other forms of assistance.
- **Address the behavior directly**: If you witness such behavior between colleagues, it may be necessary to address it directly. Let the person know that their behavior is not acceptable and that it's creating a hostile work environment.

IN GENERAL, dealing with "poking the bear" behavior requires a combination of assertiveness, communication, and emotional regulation. By staying calm, setting boundaries, and seeking support when necessary, you can effectively manage this type of behavior in a professional setting.

It is important to learn when not to respond or delay your response. There are some real tangible benefits to not responding to an email and walking over to or calling a person to discuss your reply. The power of delay allows you to clear your head and gather your thoughts. There are times when an immediate gut reaction response is not appropriate, although you feel like it is with every bone in your body with your initial response.

Sometimes you want to poke the bear. To give a curt or terse response to get under someone's skin or feel the need to be passive-aggressive. I do it, I have done it, and so does everyone else. There are times you should, and I encourage it—well, not really (I am winking at you).

What I do when I get an email that pisses me off is I click forward and ensure no one's name is in the send field. Then, I type the email I want to send and hold nothing back—curse words and all. I go all out. I get everything off my chest. I reread it and then delete it. There is this sense of freedom from my initial anger. I collect my thoughts and typically feel better.

In most cases, I will not respond to the email. If I do respond by email, it won't be for several hours. This has several benefits. First, it denies the sender a quick response. Most people say things to elicit a reaction, to get under your skin, or to just piss you off by feeling superior. Do not allow that to happen. Take control, and do not give someone easy and predictable wins. Second, it allows me to think clearly about what I want to say.

Most people are pussies, and they would never say these things to your face. They lack maturity and professionalism, but more importantly, they are cowards. Just like the trolls on social media, looking to feel superior or show they are "better" than you in some way or just to protect themselves, they lack the guts to say those things in person. To them, bringing someone down is a sport.

The worst of the bunch are those individuals who say these things behind your back and then try to reinforce them through snarky emails. They work tirelessly behind your back to undermine you, make you look bad, and reinforce their own bubbled thinking. I once hired someone like this, and sadly enough, it started well, but then she just continued to try to undermine me and drive her agenda. Ultimately, I figured out she wanted my job, and she felt that she could do it better.

What she was doing was quite apparent after I realized the two-sidedness of her communication with others. What she did not realize was that I had spent time building relationships across the organization and built trust and rapport with these key folks. So, everything she said and did eventually made it back to me. Information is power.

Once I knew what was going on, I knew I had to manage the communication and the narrative. When she would send me something, using the information I had, I was better able to control the narrative and mold things the way I wanted and never overreacted to anything she sent me. You just need to be mindful of how you respond and be able to know what is going on. Get the back story and details. More importantly, build relationships and trust with multiple people so you can get information.

The one thing I did learn from that experience is that it is hard for someone to lie to your face. When confronted, everyone (but maybe not a psychopath) will struggle to lie to your face. The truly diabolical people will have zero problems lying to your face. They are dangerous for other reasons and should be treated as such. Plus, knowing they are doing things, saying things behind your back, or purposely eliciting a response puts you in a superior position. Again, and it has been said a thousand times, knowledge is power.

Another tactic is to end passive-aggressive behavior. The best way I find to do this is awareness coupled with addressing the hot-button topics head-on. No reason to avoid topics that you know will generate issues. Just call it out early and cut off any opportunity for someone to try to undermine you. Be aggressive in addressing the concern, be open-minded, and most importantly, acknowledge the elephants in the conversion. By taking it head-on, you leave little room to maneuver for those intent on giving you heartburn. This preemptive strike prevents someone from poking the bear and disrupts their narrative and control.

To prevent accidental bear poking and to just be a better person, use your feet to communicate. I know this is getting harder and harder to do with more folks either telecommuting or working in more matrixed environments where not everyone is in the same city or office. So, getting up and walking over to talk just may not be physically possible. This is not always the case, and you should stop taking the uncomplicated way out and just sending an email. Face-to-face conversations solve a lot of problems with the keyboard courage message that tends to fly. I guess a Zoom or teams video call helps solve this as well if everyone has their camera on.

Communicating with your feet is more a mantra than a physical act. Although, if you can, you should go see someone versus sending an email. No missing intent or implied meaning. Just a conversation. This tends to clear things up quicker and defuses most situations. Unless the person is truly foolish, then you need to figure out something else to do to manage that person.

Email has been the death of real communication in a corporate environment. It has caused more angst and problems because people read too much into an email or take an email out of context. People have developed keyboard courage. They say things they normally would not say to someone's face. You see this all the time on social media. Brave keyboard warriors.

Things are better-said face to face or, if needed, by a simple phone call. I don't know how much grief I have saved myself by simply walking over or calling someone before sending an email.

Do not get me wrong, email is still needed, but using your emotional intelligence, know how the recipient may react to what you are typing. If you call ahead or walk over, explain your email face-to-face before sending it. Better yet, don't send an email at all if you can. I do know that it might not be possible, or there are multiple people on the email thread.

Catching someone off guard in email, especially if there is more than one person copied, can lead to more heartburn than it is worth. If you can frame up your message first and talk through it, there will be no surprises. Again, it is better to send less email in general. There are some real tangible benefits to sending fewer emails. One, it forces you to network internally. You also avoid inflaming an issue by having someone misunderstand the context of your reply. It further helps to get to a resolution on any outstanding questions.

Going back to the earlier section on networking internally, sending fewer emails plays right into this strategy. It gives you a reason to go over there to talk or even to call. Start with the email as the reason for the visit and weave in a "Hey, let's go to lunch." Don't use the word "sometime." Show some fortitude, and be assertive. Suggest a time: "Let's go to lunch today." If today doesn't work, nail a date down.

These opportunities are plentiful, and you need to take advantage of them. Having a face-to-face conversation with someone helps build connection, and it helps build trust. Personalize and get to know the other person.

Plus, you can read body language and recognize the tone and context of the words coming out of their mouth. You can't and never will get this from an email. It is quite the opposite. You are more likely to get it wrong.

Again, all of this helps build that personal connection

you want to build when networking. (Networking is the one thing most people do wrong. Do not be the person who gets this wrong.)

You are then able to respond at once to questions, clarify a comment, and build trust. This just doesn't happen via email. So, instead of having a back-and-forth email war, with more people added to the CC line with each reply, you can have an adult conversation that leads to more trust and connection. Then go to lunch.

I get it: Email is easy. Too easy. People tend to have this magical keyboard courage. They will say things in an email that they wouldn't dare say to someone's face. It is hard to say something that is borderline nasty when someone is looking at you. That is, of course, if you don't truly hate that person—then it is easy.

Remember, most people are pussies, and they won't say the things to your face. It is also hard to talk about someone behind their back when they are standing in front of you.

Not only will you start to earn respect, but people will also start to appreciate the effort. I mean, most people have good intentions but do not do anything about it because it is too hard or it makes them uncomfortable.

You need to get uncomfortable. It is the only way you make yourself better. The uncomfortable zone is where growth happens. If you do not push yourself or put yourself out there, you will never be more than what you are today. Trying something new is an uncomfortable place to be. Failing is an uncomfortable place to be. But it is needed, and it is the only way for you to build on yourself. You don't learn a lot when you win; you learn a tremendous amount when you lose. Failing is a possibility. Not learning from failure is not the choice. This is where growth happens. Most people fail and give up or only do what is comfortable for them. Then they wonder why they got passed over for a promotion or didn't get the cool project to work on. They never want to acknowledge that they just haven't put themselves out there and pushed hard. They sat back and, in their comfort zone, waited for someone to hand everything to them. Don't be that person.

If you stay afraid, you'll never achieve your stretch goals. Because I know you have them. Probably read it in some book or on a LinkedIn motivational post. You want to achieve important things but continue to do the same things you are doing today. Using the same playbook, not stretching yourself but convincing yourself you are, but are afraid to get uncomfortable. You won't achieve the things you want until you get out of your own head. Gary John Bishop said in his book *UnF*ck Yourself*, the person you talk to the most is yourself, and you have an uncanny ability to talk yourself out of anything. This is so true. His point was to get out of your own head and start doing. Get uncomfortable, challenge yourself, and do the things that help you achieve your goals.

Granted, this is a lot easier said than done. It is scary to go and walk into someone's office and have a potentially difficult conversation. It is uncomfortable to put yourself out there, but if you don't, you'll be the same person you are today—unachieved goals and depressed because your career feels like it is stalled. It doesn't need to be this way.

I have always been highly motivated and at times selfishly sacrificed relationships, friends, and happiness in pursuit of more money and titles. All of which are meaningless without relationships, friends, and happiness. Once you realize there is a balance between career success and the private part of your life, the better off you'll be. I know people talk about work-life balance. This has nothing to do with leaving at 5 pm or having flexibility or working flex hours. That is some millennial mumbo jumbo. What I am talking about is, you can have goals and be aggressive in trying to achieve them, but without that support and relationships, all of it is meaningless.

Does this mean you'll have to work hard or late on a project? Absolutely. Does it mean you'll have to make yourself uncomfortable? Without a doubt. But make time for those around you and build a support structure for your goals. You will enjoy the journey much more, and if you are happy personally, the work stuff comes easily.

Don't be afraid. Don't talk yourself out of goals you want to achieve because it is uncomfortable or scary. You won't grow if you don't challenge yourself. And yes, conflict and disagreements are a part of life. Do not let conflict paralyze your ability to do your job well. Give respect. Give the person creating the conflict a chance by listening and looking at conflict as an opportunity that will help you grow instead of something that you avoid at all costs. Conflict indeed creates growth if you learn from it rather than run away from it.

What I have learned throughout the years is this: Conflict doesn't kill relationships or friendships— avoidance does. If you want a relationship with someone, conflict is inevitable, and you need to be willing to work through conflict productively. I have been in many different conflict situations throughout my life. Most were resolved, but some continued when they shouldn't have because the other party was unwilling to resolve it when they could have resolved it easily. In hindsight, yes, if I had done this or that differently, maybe the conflict wouldn't have escalated as far as it did.

I was taught conflict resolution from a young age and

had forgotten about it over time. You cannot just storm into a person's office during work hours agitated and expect them to drop everything for you right then and there without saying anything else about what happened last week. You need to be able to recognize conflict, understand conflict resolution and recognize when someone is not willing to resolve conflict. But most importantly, you must know yourself well enough to realize whether you are the type of person who will resolve conflict quickly or if it will take weeks or months for you to come around.

Do you avoid conflict? Do you avoid conflict resolution? Do you let conflict last for months or years without resolving it? It is not healthy. If conflict bothers you, talk to the person who made you feel uncomfortable and constructively explain your feelings. Don't be afraid of conflict. Recognize conflict when it happens and deal with it head-on to resolve the conflict quickly. Yes, conflict does not kill relationships, but avoidance of conflict most certainly will destroy them.

Do you have de-escalation strategies that you use to turn down the temperature of a conversation? A conflict does not have to escalate if you are willing to listen and work with the person. But you must also understand conflict is a two-way street. A conflict cannot be resolved without conflict resolution from both sides. Sometimes you need to give a little, but the other side needs to give in equally for it to work.

It should be noted that conflict resolution is not solving the conflict in five steps. It does not work that way. Conflict can be solved by talking about it, but you cannot run away from conflict because conflict avoidance only creates more issues down the line. You must know yourself well enough to determine whether you are capable of conflict resolution with someone who is being combative or if you need some time to think things through before reacting.

The goal of conflict resolution is to get the situation resolved quickly while still maintaining relationships and friendships at the end of it all. If you are insistent on having your way without consideration for others, then it will make conflict resolution less likely because another person's feelings matter just as much as yours when resolving conflicts. This is especially true in the workplace.

Workplace conflict resolutions are important because of the environment it takes place in, but you need to understand conflict at work is not any different than conflict outside of work. You cannot run away from conflict or avoid conflict resolution with a combative person who will escalate conflict if you do not deal with them immediately. If your boss is constantly combative and constantly brings up old conflicts that have been resolved and constantly puts their feelings first, then you need to recognize this as a red flag and figure out how to handle the situation before it gets worse—for both parties involved.

Conflict can be healthy, but it can equally be problematic. I know that sometimes there is a natural urge to irritate people you don't like. But in the workplace, you should tread lightly. You don't want to be the one who constantly has a stick out, poking people, so to speak.

Be careful about stirring up trouble where there doesn't need to be any—even if it is tempting or if the person deserves it. If you do choose to engage in conflict, try to do so in a constructive way and be smart. Don't just aim to make the other person look bad. Focus on finding a resolution that works for everyone involved. And finally, remember that it's often better to walk away from an argument than to keep poking at it until it gets ugly. While this is sometimes fun, it can prolong things beyond what you intended.

While I can't say it enough, knowing when not to poke a bear is important. It is also important to know when to poke that bear. This includes understanding when conflict is healthy and when it is problematic. If you do choose to engage in conflict, try to do so in a constructive way.

But what do you do when someone is poking you? This is where it gets difficult. You may want to retaliate and poke back, but that can often make things worse. It's important to stay calm and try to diffuse the situation. If you can't do that, then walk away. There is no shame in admitting that you can't handle a situation and need to take a break. The goal is to avoid an escalation of the conflict.

Poking a bear can be fun, but it can also be dangerous. So be careful out there and choose your battles wisely. There are times when it is best to avoid poking a bear. I tend to poke when I have data, information, or something that supports my position. For me, this is making sure my stick is pointy enough. The emotionally immature tend not to handle conflict well, just heading into it blindly. But keep calm, don't overreact or lash out. Be prepared and know when to poke back.

3

OFFICE PREPPER

Are you an office prepper? Cubical Survivalist? Do you know how to survive in the office environment? Have any idea what that means? Probably not. This isn't a simple question of just showing up. That is not surviving. An office prepper is someone who tries to be prepared— prepared to deal with different personalities, prepared to deal with projects that don't go as planned, and prepared to deal with the inevitable curve ball that will come your way. Whether it comes from a co-worker, your manager, or a peer, being prepared to deal with whatever comes your way is essential.

Getting to know the people you work with and how they react to good and unwelcome news will help you be prepared. Knowledge is power. The more you know about those around you, the better off you will be and the greater likelihood you will be successful. You can then use this knowledge to your advantage.

This idea of being an office prepper goes beyond just having and using knowledge. It also applies to thinking ahead for any situation you are walking into, like a presentation. Maybe you are walking into a client meeting or a sales presentation, but have you done enough to be ready for it?

I tend to research the people I am meeting outside of my organization before meeting with them. Do we have mutual connections? Who and how are we connected? What is in their background that I can relate to, something I can use as an icebreaker? Maybe it's information I can use to connect with a person on a personal level.

Do you prepare to sell your idea to key decision-makers before a broader audience? You don't ever want to blindside your manager or key stakeholders. It never goes the way want if you do. You need to get buy-in from a key individual(s) and avoid and beat back any naysayers. This way, you won't spend the whole time trying to convince everyone.

Think back to the pack mentality. If something is going south, people pile on. If it is going well, the same occurs. By getting it sold prior, the rest of the group comes around a lot easier.

Here's another concept: Two is one, one is none. I have heard survivalists and doomsday preppers say it, and it applies in the business world as well. But what does the phrase two is one, and one is none mean? In its most basic form, it means to be prepared by having more than one choice or solution, like bringing printed copies of your presentation just in case the projector doesn't work. It means having a plan A but also having a plan B ready to roll.

When you go to a job interview, do you bring extra copies of your resume in case the interviewer can't find the copy that HR gave them? Do you do background research on the people you are meeting with? All of this is the mindset of an office prepper.

The truth is, things go wrong, things break or don't

work, ideas get shot down, and you just need to be prepared when things go wrong. You can't be in a client meeting and have a client shoot down an idea and not have ideas two, three, and four ready to go.

Sometimes a preemptive strike is needed, but note that some folks will get blindsided. You just need to be prepared to deal with it. I recall a situation at one job where my department was getting pushback from another department. There was a tense meeting, and what I knew was an inevitable run to my manager to tell on me. Not one to panic, I knew what was going to happen before it happened. I was prepared. What others did not know was I already knew how the meeting was going to unfold. There were telltale signs before. My intuition told me so. Because I was emotionally aware, I noticed what others were saying a few days before the meltdown meeting.

So being emotionally aware and an office prepper, I had all the tools and knowledge I needed. I took what I knew and the plan I had for the meeting and met with my manager to explain the background, the current situation, and what exactly I was going to do and say. I also provided reasoning and expected results. This was all rounded out with what I expected as pushback and who I expected to come to my manager to complain.

I cut off all avenues to "get me." My manager was fully prepared for what was coming, with no surprises. Plus, they had all the details, background, reasoning, etc. So when the inevitable complaint came, I already had support. I knew I did. I was confident in the meltdown meeting. I got agreement about my plan well before the meeting.

Not only that, but I also had plans B and C if the meltdown meeting happened not to go as I expected. I was well prepared no matter which way the meeting went, and my manager was not only aware of what I planned to do; I got buy-in for the plan. So, any pushback would be met with someone who not only was aware of what I was doing, they agreed with it!

It pays to be prepared, and it is hard to be thrown under a bus if you own the bus, you are driving the bus, you know the route the bus will take, and you set the schedule on which the bus will run. The common theme is knowledge, and I cannot stress this enough, the best information is going to come from the relationships you build and the trust you have earned.

If you are not a trusted individual, you are going to be at a disadvantage. Build those relationships and have a good working relationship not only in your immediate area but across the organization. Be a known entity.

When you are thinking about being that office prepper, again, you need to think, why have one when you can have two at less than twice the cost? Going back to what I said earlier, the other common saying when it comes to prepping is one is none, and two is one. Have more than one choice for any one problem. Have more than one advocate. Have more than one champion. Basically, have more than one of anything when thinking about office prepping.

This leads to asking who you can rally to your cause. What internal networking have you done to get people on your side? Who have you built trust with, and more importantly, who do you trust?

These are not easy things to do, but they are very necessary. It requires deliberate action on your part to look for, find, and build these relationships. You need to effectively network both internally and externally.

You need to elevate yourself, make it known what you are capable of and how you can help others. This comes with risks. Aligning yourself with the wrong people could do more damage to your reputation and your personal brand. You need to approach this with a trust but verify mentality. Selectively build these relationships and remember it is a two-way street. You need to give as much as you take. Be strategic about it and navigate with awareness.

So, now that you are a prepared office prepper, there is one important rule you need to follow, and it is simple: Assume management has only half the story. To think that someone even one level above you, let alone two levels or more, is in the weeds, you are sadly mistaken.

There are always exceptions to this rule, and if senior management is in the weeds, you have a completely different problem, and I would suggest looking for a new job. It is not sustainable to have the CEO making keyword decisions. And yes, that is a true story.

I know it begs the question of why a CEO would be that far into the weeds, but if that is the case, no level of prepping is going to solve the core issues at that organization. It screams lack of trust, lack of hiring qualified people to do their jobs, and it drives out good talent because who the hell needs that every day?

So, let's assume you don't have a senior leader deep in the weeds. You need to be prepared to communicate with the leadership, knowing that they may know little to nothing about the story you are trying to tell. That means you must be brief. Zero fluff.

Not only do they not know everything, but they also don't care about all the details. I was coaching someone on my team once and told him to draft the email status and send it to me for review. My only comment back was, "Cut the copy by fifty percent."

I didn't even read it; I just cut the words by 50%. He sent back another draft, and I said, "Cut the word count again." And again, I didn't even read it. Got the final copy back, and I read it. It was very concise and to the point.

People tend to think that more is better when communicating. Nothing could be further from the truth, especially when dealing with business executives. The same could be said about PowerPoint. More is definitely not better. This could be a whole other book in and of itself.

When you start to formulate your message, make sure you only deal with facts. Anything extra or miscellaneous details or individual disagreements or dynamics, just leave it out. It is not needed, not helpful, and a waste of time. Cut to the chase. This leads to my next point.

Make sure you tell your side of the story briefly. It is okay to state your position but deal in facts and only give opinions when appropriate. It is important to make sure you help drive the narrative without being too political. Sometimes it is unavoidable to insert office politics; just be smart about it. I talk about office politics in depth in a later chapter since it is a topic that merits its own chapter. The biggest takeaway here is to be concise, state your position, and support it with facts and solid rationale.

One of the key goals here is managing up. Manage the communication, manage the narrative, and show them you are the leader you are or want to be. Good management wants, needs, and desires people who will challenge the status quo. They hate yes people. The only managers who like "yes people" are bad managers. I am not talking about just being the devil's advocate every time; I am talking about expressing your thoughts on better ways to do things. Just don't agree with the boss. Sucking up to bad managers might get you promoted, but it is just going to make you a bad manager. You may achieve your goals but at a cost.

The one thing that is vitally important to know is just because someone is in management or a senior leader or is a "founder" doesn't make them a smart person. Granted, some are very smart people, and others are plain dumb.

They happen to be in their position and have no talent or capability to be a leader. Some get there by pure luck or by joining at the right time. But having CEO, CRO, CMO, or COO in their title doesn't make them special. I have seen one too many "leaders" who should be leaders in those positions. You must live with this fact and plan accordingly.

Some of these leaders are only as good as what is fed to them. So be the person who is driving your thought process and be the provider of information that helps drive your narrative.

Because if you don't do this, someone else will. And the person who is feeding them may not be a support or champion, and as I said earlier, they have their own agenda. In the next chapter, I will talk more about the Us vs. Them or, more accurately, them vs. you.

But digging deeper into the concept of managing up, let's explore how it can help you. Managing up is the art of effectively communicating with your superiors to ensure that you are on the same page and that your priorities align with theirs. It is a crucial concept in the workplace, especially if you want to advance your career or navigate challenging situations.

As an office prepper, managing up is an essential skill to develop. By effectively managing up, you can ensure that your boss is aware of your contributions, understands the challenges you face, and is aligned with your goals. This way, you can avoid being blindsided by last-minute changes, and you can be proactive in anticipating and addressing issues before they become major problems.

Managing up also enables you to demonstrate your value to the organization and establish yourself as a trusted advisor to your boss. By building a positive working relationship, you can gain the trust and confidence of your superiors and be seen as a valuable asset to the team.

Furthermore, managing up can help you gain insight into your manager's priorities, goals, and work style. By understanding what your manager values and how they prefer to work, you can tailor your approach to align with their preferences and increase your chances of success.

Overall, managing up is a powerful tool for office preppers who want to be prepared and successful in the workplace. It allows you to build strong relationships with your superiors, gain insight into their priorities, and establish yourself as a valuable asset to the team. By mastering the art of managing up, you can achieve your career goals while maintaining a positive and productive working relationship with your boss.

You need to be a Kool-Aid Drinker in public and a Svengali in private. How do you manage trying to push through change when your management is only interested in you doing what has already been laid out to you? How does this change when the leadership will potentially label you as unengaged if you publicly push back or don't toe the line? This is particularly difficult if you don't buy into the plan or strategy and especially difficult when you know there is a better way to achieve the same or better results.

This comes back to driving the narrative and controlling what you can control and, at a minimum, influencing what you cannot control to the best of your ability.

But this also means you need to swallow a bitter pill now

and then to ensure you can stay on the right side of the leader. This doesn't mean you become a yes man.

It means you must become that silent influencer. It means you must build trust and build a support base of your peers. It is not easy, but some toxic environments require you to skillfully navigate and balance your way through this obstacle.

But sometimes, being an office prepper has to do with being prepared when you are not the smartest person in the room.

When you are not the smartest person in the room, you must be prepared. You can't just sit back and hope that someone else will do the work for you. You must be ready to put in the extra effort to make sure that you are prepared.

There are a few things that you can do to make sure that you are prepared at work. First, you need to make sure that you are always learning.

You should never stop learning new things. Even if you feel like you know everything, there is always something new to learn. Second, you need to be willing to ask questions. If you don't understand something, ask questions.

Don't be afraid to look stupid. It's better to ask questions and look stupid than to not ask questions and be unprepared. Third, you need to be organized. This one is especially important if you are not the smartest person in the room. You need to make sure that you have your ducks in a row so that you can be prepared for anything that comes your way.

If you follow these tips, you will be prepared at work even if you are not the smartest person in the room. Just remember to always keep learning, be willing to ask questions, and be organized. With these tips, you'll be prepared for anything that comes your way.

The key is also to anticipate what is needed. Does your manager always ask the same questions? Does he bring up a concern in another meeting? Use that to reinforce a common theme. Shows you are listening. Demonstrates that you are solutions-oriented.

You will not always be the smartest person in the room, but if you are prepared, you can fake it until you make it. If you have this type of resiliency, resourcefulness, and scrappiness, it will make you a powerful player. You would just need to deliver on your tasks and projects. Then couple this with managing up, providing detailed but not overly detailed communication, and you will be better prepared to excel.

In this chapter, the concept of being an "office prepper" is introduced as someone who is prepared to deal with different personalities, projects that don't go as planned, and unexpected curveballs that may come their way. It is essential to be emotionally aware and know how to think ahead in any situation, like a presentation or a client meeting.

The key is to have more than one choice or solution, to be well-prepared no matter which way the meeting goes, and to assume that management has only half the story.

It is also vital to manage communication, tell your side of the story briefly and with facts, and be a Kool-Aid Drinker in public and a Svengali in private. Finally, the chapter emphasizes the importance of always learning, asking questions, being organized, and anticipating what is needed to be better prepared for anything that comes your way.

Being an office prepper also involves building strong relationships and trust within the organization, knowing who to rally to your cause, and being strategic about networking both internally and externally. It's important to challenge the status quo, express your thoughts on better ways to do things, and avoid being a "yes person" to bad managers. You must plan accordingly and skillfully navigate toxic environments to stay on the right side of the leader without compromising your integrity.

The concept of being an office prepper is all about being prepared for any situation that may arise in the workplace, whether it's dealing with difficult personalities or unexpected changes in projects. By following the tips and strategies mentioned in this chapter, you can position yourself as a powerful player in your organization and achieve your career goals while maintaining your integrity and professionalism.

4

IT IS US VS. THEM

A nd more accurately, it is them vs. you.

Replace "them" with any department or, for that matter, any person, even in your own department. Ignore any leader or HR person who says, "It is not us versus them," when referring to conflict between people or departments. I call bull. Everyone has an agenda, especially those who say they don't. Sometimes the most dangerous are the people in your own department or peers.

The idea of having friends at work is great and makes the time go by more easily, especially on projects. But at the end of the day, they are in it for themselves. They want to be recognized, rewarded, and promoted. Further, they do not want someone else to get those things, especially you. This is not to sound negative, or maybe it is, but it is the truth.

Everyone's goals do not align and never will. I never understood how they could align. Granted, the company can have overarching goals, such as being a top internal retailer, but it is broad enough that it is all-encompassing. But very rarely are people thinking in such terms, and as if it is instinctual, they always personalize it.

It is about them. It is about what is in it for them—and how they can get recognition or rewards or bonuses or a promotion. This is terrible, but it is a common occurrence.

Revenue is everyone's problem. It is just that each department has its own self-interested goals in how it gets there. Individuals have their own self-interest in how to get there. These competing interests cause conflict and misalignment.

So, while you push one idea, someone could be pushing another. Sometimes it is personal, such as a person not liking you, but most of the time, it is not personal—it is selfish. People want what's best for them and not you or anyone else. Now amplify this across the board, and it is a scene right out of *Mad Max*.

The people you manage are against you. They want your job; they think they can do it better than you can. They will undermine you. I recall a time when I hired a very smart individual to help grow a marketing team. Everything started fine, but I figured that they were just getting their sea legs and oriented to the organization. Over time, the behind-my-back conversations about how I am bad at my job and how this individual could do it better and differently increased.

Again, my network and relationships gave me the inside track of what was going on. Even several of the other members of my team came to me, mostly out to protect themselves.

So, you see, sometimes the enemy is from within, someone you gave a chance to and wanted to trust. It is important to keep your head on a swivel and know that people looking to undermine you aren't necessarily from other departments and could be the person next door.

But what does that mean, and why should you care? It

means that even the people you would expect to be on your side are not necessarily going to be, and you need to adjust your management style, have self-awareness, and be proactive in tamping down any possible revolt. The revolt is likely to come even from the most unlikely people.

Make sure you communicate the positives for them and give folks the credit when it is deserved. Just be mindful of people's behavior and their end goals and that there will be conflicting priorities. Companies promote, "We are a team," and yes, to some extent, it is true, but all too often, you are competing against folks who wouldn't mind taking you down to make themselves look better.

It is all about me—or so it seems. People are self-interested, and their end game is what is in it for them. For example, if you ask someone to do something that will move an agenda forward but not be directly related to promoting themselves, they will look at this as a distraction from their personal objectives and likely decline the opportunity. Again, it may seem like no big deal because they declined or rejected your request, but what you don't see is the stories they tell behind your back about how distracted they are by another project. Do you see where I am going with this?

There have been many examples of this over my career across many companies and industries. It isn't just retail. This is something that hit home for me when I was at this global Fortune 500 company. We had a lot of attrition—good employees leaving the company—, and it just wasn't adding up until one day, after someone turned down an opportunity to work on something else, they told me why. They said, "I have my own agenda, and if this takes off, you are going to get all the credit, so I am declining your offer." My first response was, "Are you kidding?"

How about teamwork...the company...? But then you realize that is not how other people work. They don't think like that. You need to understand that these people are selfish and motivated by what is in it for them. Let me tell you this if you have a team member who is only about what's in it for them and doesn't seem to grasp teamwork—or even worse, they don't care: They will do more damage than good.

I know that it may be hard to talk about how to make teamwork work when people don't want to play nice with others. A lot of times, this type of behavior is because people are not used to having their ideas challenged, or they don't like to be held accountable. It is important to make sure you give them the respect of presenting their ideas with thoughtful feedback but in a respectful way. This doesn't mean you need to accept everything they say, but it does mean that when your team member has an idea or suggestion, even if it isn't perfect, acknowledge it and thank them for their input. If you don't do this, then they will not trust you and feel like they can't approach you with any ideas for fear of doing something wrong.

Trust your gut! People are good at hiding things or sugarcoating things to get what they want, so pay attention to body language, facial expressions, and tone of voice. If an employee seems to be happy about something, but they don't seem very excited, then your Spidey sense should start tingling because that could mean their real motivation is different—maybe it isn't teamwork at all, maybe they are just trying to look like a team player.

This also means you need to listen closely to what people say and pay attention to the inflection in their voice and their body language. It isn't always easy, but if you suspect someone doesn't want teamwork, you need to follow up with them and ask them why. You shouldn't necessarily expect a straight answer, but listen more intently for other clues, like avoiding eye contact or remaining quiet when others are speaking.

Some people may also feel like they are not doing teamwork because they don't see the big picture as you do—that is, you know how it all fits together. You need to make sure that your employees understand their role in teamwork. This will help them understand their responsibilities and where teamwork fits into what they are responsible for. If you find yourself wondering why some of your team members aren't more engaged teamwork-wise, or if you even think they don't want teamwork at all, then I would highly recommend getting an outside set of eyes on the situation. Maybe get a trusted peer or even human resources to have a look.

If someone is avoiding teamwork altogether but still wants credit for working hard, look out! It is always you versus them. If teamwork is important to you, then teamwork must also be important to them. It doesn't matter if teamwork is their main motivation for doing good work. If teamwork isn't what they really care about, but they are just looking out for themselves—that won't last. They will eventually realize that teamwork will help them do better work, and then they will embrace teamwork as well.

What can you do?

Make sure you show your employees how teamwork can benefit them more than if they were trying to go at things on their own. This may take some time and effort on your part but trust me, it's worth it.

Give constructive feedback when an employee has done something wrong or subpar. Pointing out someone's mistakes directly but politely is a great way to show team-work and help them grow.

Point out when you have noticed good teamwork from your employees, so they know it isn't just about doing things well individually but that it's also about working together to get the best possible result. People love positive reinforcement!

If you suspect an employee may not want teamwork, then follow up with them. Ask them if everything is okay since they seem stressed lately. Ask if something has changed recently because their behavior seems different than before. Don't make it sound like an accusation, though, or they will feel like teamwork talk is always about them, and they will start to resent it.

Remind your employees that teamwork does not mean teamwork, teamwork, teamwork all the time. It's easy to forget about other important things sometimes, and getting reminders can be very helpful.

Tell your employees that teamwork doesn't always have to come with sugarcoating or stabbing people in the back. Teamwork isn't coercive or self-righteous, either. It simply means working together for a common goal without under-mining each other or keeping secrets from one another as much as possible.

Try using different communication when dealing with different people. If teamwork is most important with your peers/team members, then use teamwork talk more often. If teamwork isn't as huge of a priority, then reduce the amount of teamwork-talk you use on that person. Being able to change the way you communicate is a great skill to have and will allow teamwork-talk to flow more naturally without coming off as job interview talk. It's all about knowing your audience and how they function best!

Use some teamwork-talk yourself as often as possible. At least try not to avoid teamwork altogether, as some people do. It can be easy to forget about something, but once you start reminding others, they will follow suit, and everyone will be very thankful for it!

Teams and projects often create office politics and difficult people, which can be a challenge in any workplace or for any project. However, being prepared can help you navigate these situations with greater ease and confidence. Here are some steps you can take to be prepared:

- **Know your worth and stand up for yourself**: When dealing with difficult people, it's important to have a clear understanding of your value and to be confident in your abilities. This will help you to stand up for yourself and professionally assert yourself.
- **Develop strong relationships**: Building strong relationships with colleagues and superiors can help you navigate office politics more effectively. These relationships can provide you with support and a sounding board when dealing with difficult people and challenging situations.
- **Stay informed**: Keeping up to date with workplace news and changes can help you anticipate potential challenges and be prepared to deal with them. Try to network with colleagues and attend internal meetings to stay informed.
- **Be professional**: Regardless of the situation, it's important to maintain a professional demeanor. This means avoiding gossip, being respectful and

polite, and avoiding engaging in negative
behavior.

- **Seek support**: If you're struggling with a difficult
person or situation, don't hesitate to seek support
from colleagues, a mentor, or HR. Talking to
someone outside of the situation can help you
gain perspective and come up with a plan for how
to handle it.

MANAGING priorities among colleagues in the same
department can be a challenging task, but it is crucial for
the success of the team and the organization. One of the key
things to keep in mind when dealing with conflicting priorities is open communication. Encouraging team members
to share their priorities and concerns can help prevent
misunderstandings and ensure that everyone is on the same
page.

Another important step is to establish a clear system for
prioritization. This can include setting goals, deadlines, and
metrics for success. By having a shared understanding of
what needs to be accomplished (and when), team members
can more easily prioritize their tasks and avoid conflicts.

Inevitably, there will be times when team members have
conflicting priorities or need to make difficult decisions
about which tasks to prioritize. In these situations, it can be
helpful to involve a neutral party, such as a supervisor or
manager. This person can provide guidance and help facilitate discussions to find a solution that works for everyone.

It's also important to be flexible and adaptable. Priorities
can shift and change quickly, so team members need to be
prepared to pivot as needed. By staying agile and open to
change, team members can more effectively manage

competing priorities and maintain a positive and productive work environment.

Overall, managing priorities among colleagues in the same department requires a combination of communication, clear prioritization systems, and flexibility. By working together and staying focused on the goals of the team and organization, team members can successfully navigate conflicts and achieve success.

When it comes to managing priorities between people in different departments, the challenges can be even greater. There may be differences in goals, timelines, and even communication styles that can make it difficult to find common ground. However, several strategies can help bridge the gap and foster productive collaboration.

First and foremost, communication is key. It's important to establish regular check-ins and open lines of communication with colleagues in other departments. This can help ensure that everyone is aware of each other's priorities and can collaborate effectively.

Another important strategy is to align goals and metrics across departments. By establishing shared goals and measures of success, team members can work towards a common purpose and avoid conflicts. This can also help promote accountability and ensure that everyone is working towards the same result.

It's also important to be flexible and adaptable when dealing with priorities across departments. There may be unexpected shifts in priorities or changes in the business environment that require quick action. By staying agile and open to change, team members can more effectively manage competing priorities and work towards common goals.

In some cases, it may be necessary to involve higher-level managers or executives to help resolve conflicts between departments. These leaders can help provide guidance and facilitate discussions to find solutions that work for everyone.

Overall, managing priorities between people in different departments requires a combination of communication, alignment, flexibility, and collaboration. By working together towards common goals and staying focused on the needs of the business, team members can successfully navigate competing priorities and achieve success.

By following these steps, you can be better prepared for office politics and difficult people in the workplace. Remember, it's important to maintain your integrity, stay calm, and approach situations with a level head. With practice and patience, you'll be able to handle office politics and difficult people with ease.

But is all competition bad in the workplace? Competition in the workplace can have both positive and negative impacts on employee performance, particularly when it comes to competing priorities. On the one hand, healthy competition can motivate employees to work harder and more efficiently, leading to increased productivity and better performance. However, on the other hand, excessive competition or an overly competitive culture can have negative effects on employee morale and job satisfaction, ultimately leading to poorer performance.

When it comes to competing priorities, competition can create a sense of urgency and drive employees to work more efficiently and effectively. However, this can also lead to a "win at all costs" mentality, where employees may prioritize their own goals over the needs of the team or the organization. This can lead to conflicts between colleagues and departments, as well as missed opportunities for collaboration and shared success.

Excessive competition in the workplace can have several negative effects on employees and the overall organization. One of the key negative impacts is increased stress and anxiety among employees. When competition is seen as the primary driver of success, employees may feel pressured to constantly outperform their colleagues and meet ever-increasing expectations. This can lead to burnout, anxiety, and other negative impacts on mental health and well-being.

Another negative impact of excessive competition is decreased collaboration and teamwork. When employees feel like they are competing against one another, they may be less likely to share information, resources, or ideas with their colleagues. This can lead to missed opportunities for collaboration and innovation, as well as silos and barriers between departments or teams.

Excessive competition can also lead to a "me-first" mentality among employees. When competition is the primary motivator, employees may prioritize their own goals and success over the needs of the team or the organization. This can lead to conflicts between colleagues and departments, as well as missed opportunities for shared success.

Finally, excessive competition can have negative impacts on employee morale and job satisfaction. When employees feel like they are constantly in competition with their colleagues, it can create a tense and stressful work environment. This can lead to decreased job satisfaction and increased turnover, as employees may feel like they need to leave the organization to escape the negative impacts of competition.

Overall, while competition can be a powerful motivator, employers need to balance it with collaboration, teamwork, and a focus on shared goals. By promoting a culture of healthy competition and teamwork, employers can help employees work towards common priorities and achieve success while also maintaining a positive and supportive work environment.

5

7 HELPFUL TIPS CONCERNING TEAMWORK

Teamwork is a critical component of any successful workplace, but it can be challenging to cultivate a culture that fosters collaboration and mutual support. In this chapter, we will explore seven tips for promoting teamwork in the workplace, including how to approach teamwork from different perspectives, the importance of making teamwork enjoyable, and the benefits of encouraging individual initiative when it is necessary.

By adopting these strategies, you can help create a more cohesive and productive team that works together effectively towards shared goals.

I will discuss how to motivate team members to embrace teamwork and how to navigate situations where teamwork may not always be the best approach. From emphasizing the personal benefits of teamwork to incorporating fun and games into teamwork-talk, these tips will help you create a workplace where collaboration and cooperation thrive.

One important aspect of promoting teamwork is understanding that different individuals may have different perspectives on what it means to work as a team. By considering everyone's point of view and valuing their input, you can create a more inclusive and effective team that leverages the unique skills and insights of each member.

I will also explore how to balance the need for teamwork with the need for individual initiative and leadership. While teamwork is essential for many tasks, there may be times when a single person needs to take control of a situation or make a decision on their own. By acknowledging these situations and encouraging team members to take responsibility for their actions, you can help build a culture of trust and accountability that supports both teamwork and individual growth.

Overall, I aim to provide practical advice and insights that will help you cultivate a workplace culture that values and promotes effective teamwork. By leveraging these tips and strategies, you can create a team that works together seamlessly, supports each other, and achieves great results.

With that, here are Seven Helpful Tips to make teamwork work for you.

1. When doing teamwork- talk with others, always consider their perspective and think about how they may feel. Don't just assume that because teamwork is teamwork you know what teamwork means to them—it just isn't true!

2. Let your employees get used to teamwork- talk before moving on to other teamwork topics. Don't jump from one thing to another too quickly without giving teamwork a chance. This will allow both of you time to bond over teamwork as

well as learn more about each other's opinions on teamwork.

3. If you have someone who doesn't seem interested in teamwork, then focus on telling them why teamwork is good for them first, not the group or the company. Once teamwork is important to them as an individual, teamwork will become a lot more relevant to everyone else who hears teamwork-talk from that person.

4. To really push teamwork into the workplace once and for all, teamwork needs to be fun! A fantastic way to do this is by including teamwork activities in mandatory corporate events, Just make sure they're not too strict, or people may feel like teamwork is unnecessarily forced on them. If you want teamwork to stay, then it must be wanted— remember that!

5. Remind employees that teamwork doesn't always mean someone has to take complete control of everything. Teamwork means giving up some control but also taking responsibility when something goes wrong so both can learn from their mistakes together.

6. Make teamwork-talk a game. Don't make it seem like work at all! Mix teamwork-talk with jokes and lighthearted banter to create teamwork fun for everyone.

7. Teamwork is supposed to be teamwork, but teamwork isn't always the right answer. Sometimes, one person should pull through or take control of a situation even though teamwork might be more helpful. It's not personal, either. Teamwork may hinder someone's ability to lead

during a specific time because they're simply better suited for that purpose.

TEAMWORK IS crucial in any project, as it allows individuals with diverse skills to work together towards a common goal. An effective team can bring out the best in its members, leading to increased motivation and better results. However, forming and maintaining an effective team can be a challenge, especially when working with people who have different personalities, work styles, and objectives.

To make teams more effective, it is important to start with clear and well-defined goals. This will help team members understand what they are working towards and how their tasks contribute to the success of the project. It is also important to establish clear roles and responsibilities, as well as a line of communication that allows everyone to stay informed and engaged.

Another key aspect of effective teamwork is building trust and promoting a positive work culture. This can be done by encouraging open and honest communication, recognizing individual contributions, and fostering a sense of belonging and shared purpose among team members. Regular team-building activities can also help to strengthen relationships and increase cohesiveness.

Effective teams also rely on strong leadership, as well as individuals who are willing to take responsibility for their actions and work together to overcome challenges. It is also important to have systems in place to track progress, adjust as needed, and celebrate successes along the way.

Effective teamwork requires a combination of clear goals, open communication, trust, leadership, and a positive work culture. By focusing on these elements, project teams can work more effectively and achieve better results.

While teamwork is essential for successful projects, several pitfalls can derail even the best-intentioned teams. Some of the common pitfalls of teams and teamwork include the following:

- **Lack of clarity:** Teams can struggle when goals and expectations are unclear, leading to confusion and miscommunication. To avoid this, it is important to establish clear objectives and expectations at the outset of the project.
- **Poor communication:** Effective communication is crucial for teams to work together effectively. Teams can break down when there are misunderstandings, missed deadlines, or a lack of accountability. Regular check-ins, open lines of communication, and clear documentation can help mitigate these issues.
- **Lack of trust:** When team members do not trust each other, it can lead to defensive behavior and decreased collaboration. To build trust, it is important to foster an open and honest work environment, encourage transparency, and acknowledge and address conflicts when they arise.
- **Inadequate leadership:** Teams need strong leadership to guide them and provide direction. A lack of leadership, or poor leadership, can result in confusion and lack of direction, leading to

project delays and decreased motivation among
team members.

- **Resistance to change:** Teams can become
resistant to change, which can impact their ability
to adapt to new circumstances and overcome
challenges. To avoid this, it is important to
involve team members in decision-making
processes and clearly communicate the reasons
for changes.

BY BEING aware of these pitfalls and taking proactive steps
to avoid them, project teams can work more effectively and
achieve better results. This includes establishing clear goals,
promoting open communication, building trust, providing
strong leadership, and being open to change.

Improving communication within a team is critical for
successful collaboration and achieving project goals. Here
are some strategies for improving communication in
teamwork:

- **Establish clear communication channels**.
Teams should establish clear and consistent
channels for communication, such as regular
team meetings, email, or messaging platforms.
This helps to ensure that everyone is on the same
page and that information is shared in a timely
manner.
- **Encourage open and honest communication**.
Teams should create an environment where team
members feel comfortable sharing their thoughts,

ideas, and concerns. Encouraging open and honest communication helps to build trust and fosters a sense of collaboration.

- **Clarify roles and responsibilities**. Teams should clearly define each person's role and responsibilities to prevent misunderstandings and miscommunication.
- **Foster active listening**. When team members listen attentively to what others are saying, it can help improve communication and reduce misunderstandings.
- **Encourage feedback**. Teams should encourage regular feedback from all team members, both positive and constructive. This helps to improve communication and fosters a culture of continuous improvement.
- **Use visual aids**. Charts, diagrams, or presentations can help to clarify complex information and improve understanding.
- **Celebrating successes**. Both big and small. It can help improve communication and foster a positive team spirit.

By taking these steps, teams can improve their communication and work more effectively together toward project success.

Strong leadership is essential for project teams to achieve success. A strong leader sets the tone for the team, provides direction and guidance, and helps to create a positive work environment. Here are some of the key ways in which strong leadership can benefit project teams:

- **Provides direction:** A strong leader provides a clear vision for the project and communicates it effectively to the team. This helps to ensure that everyone is working towards the same goal and that the project is progressing in the right direction.
- **Motivates the team:** Strong leaders can inspire and motivate team members, increasing their engagement and commitment to the project.
- **Encourages collaboration:** Good leaders foster an environment of collaboration, encouraging team members to work together to achieve common goals.
- **Addresses challenges:** Strong leaders are proactive in addressing challenges that may arise during a project, helping to keep the team on track and focused on success.
- **Promotes accountability:** Good leaders hold team members accountable for their actions, ensuring that everyone is pulling their weight and contributing to the project's success.
- **Fosters a positive work culture:** A strong leader sets the tone for the team, creating a positive and productive work environment that encourages teamwork and collaboration.

STRONG LEADERSHIP IS essential for project teams to achieve success. A strong leader provides direction, motivation, support and helps to create a positive work culture that encourages teamwork and collaboration. By having strong leadership, project teams can overcome challenges, achieve their goals, and deliver successful projects.

While teamwork can bring many benefits, it's important to be aware of the potential pitfalls that can arise when working in a group. One common issue is the lack of clear goals and direction. Without a clearly defined objective, team members may become confused about their responsibilities, which can lead to frustration, conflict, and even project failure.

Another potential challenge is communication breakdowns. Even when everyone has the best intentions, misunderstandings and miscommunications can occur, leading to delays, mistakes, and overall inefficiency. It's important to establish a communication plan that ensures everyone is on the same page and has access to the information they need to do their job effectively.

Personality clashes and differences in work styles can also create friction within a team. While diversity can be a strength, it's important to address conflicts early and proactively to prevent them from escalating.

Finally, ineffective leadership can also be a significant pitfall. A leader who is unable to inspire and motivate their team, or who lacks the skills and knowledge needed to guide the project to success, can create a negative work environment and undermine the team's effectiveness.

By being aware of these potential pitfalls and taking steps to address them proactively, project teams can build a culture of trust, open communication, and collaboration that allows everyone to work together effectively towards a common goal.

Teamwork can bring many benefits to a project and its team members. First and foremost, when individuals work together as a team, they can leverage each other's diverse skills and perspectives to achieve better results than they could individually. This can lead to increased innovation, creativity, and problem-solving capabilities.

Working in a team can also provide a sense of support and motivation, as individuals can rely on each other for help and encouragement when needed. This can foster a positive work environment that promotes mutual respect, trust, and a shared sense of purpose.

Effective teamwork can also lead to increased efficiency and productivity, as team members can divide the workload according to their strengths and work together to ensure that deadlines are met. Additionally, when individuals work in a team, they can learn from each other and develop new skills, which can benefit both the project and their personal and professional growth.

Finally, when a project is successful due to effective teamwork, it can be a source of pride and accomplishment for all team members. Celebrating success together can further strengthen the bonds between team members and promote a positive work culture that encourages future collaboration and success.

Overall, teamwork can bring many benefits, including increased innovation, support and motivation, efficiency and productivity, personal and professional growth, and a sense of accomplishment and pride. By leveraging these benefits, project teams can achieve better results and create a positive work environment that promotes success and growth for all team members.

Teamwork can have both positive and negative aspects. While effective teamwork can bring benefits such as increased innovation, support and motivation, efficiency, personal and professional growth, and a sense of accomplishment, there are potential pitfalls such as unclear goals, communication breakdowns, personality clashes, and ineffective leadership.

By being aware of these challenges and addressing them proactively, project teams can create a positive work environment that promotes mutual respect, trust, and collaboration, leading to better results and personal and professional growth for all team members.

6

3 UNHELPFUL TIPS CONCERNING TEAMWORK

Teamwork is often considered the cornerstone of success in the workplace. But what happens when someone says they aren't interested in it? It's tempting to push the issue, to try to convince them of its importance. However, this approach could do more harm than good. After all, if someone isn't on board with the idea of teamwork, can it truly be considered teamwork at all? In this chapter, we'll explore the importance of voluntary participation in teamwork and how forcing the issue could backfire.

It's easy to spot the benefits of teamwork—increased productivity, better communication, and a greater sense of community in the workplace. But not everyone may be as enthusiastic about the idea. So, how can you encourage teamwork without coming across as overbearing? The key is to approach the subject with tact and consideration. In this chapter, I'll explore the nuances of introducing teamwork to those who may benefit from it and how to do so without being pushy.

Teamwork is an essential component of any successful

organization. But how do you talk about it without resorting to buzzwords and jargon? Avoiding teamwork-talk entirely may seem like a good idea, but it can actually do more harm than good. In this chapter, I'll explore how to talk about teamwork in a way that's clear and concise, so everyone in the workplace can understand its importance and their role in making it a success.

We've all heard the saying, "There's no 'I' in 'team'," but what happens when someone tries to make it all about them? It's an all-too-common scenario in the workplace—someone tries to use teamwork to gain control or undermine someone else's authority. In this chapter, I'll explore why this approach is not only unhelpful but also counter-productive. I'll also provide tips on how to approach teamwork in a way that benefits everyone involved.

Here are the Three Unhelpful Tips to avoid when dealing with teamwork:

1. If someone says they aren't interested in teamwork, then leave them alone.
2. If there's someone you think may benefit from teamwork more than others, then it's okay to bring teamwork to that person's attention; however, don't be aggressive about teamwork or teamwork talk. The idea is to encourage teamwork, not make every conversation about teamwork.
3. Don't do something like dancing around teamwork by avoiding teamwork jargon entirely. This will confuse everyone and make teamwork seem unreliable at best because no one knows

what anyone else means when they say something with "teamwork" in it. Just saying, "We need another person for this," or "You're doing great work here," tells people a lot more about how you feel specifically than staying away from teamwork-talk does.

HERE IS a fourth unhelpful tip to avoid when dealing with teamwork: Don't try teamwork to get ahead. Teamwork can only help you when teamwork is something wanted by everyone in the workplace. Teamwork isn't a way to take control of a situation or undermine someone else's authority.

Teamwork is an important aspect of any successful workplace, but it must be approached with sensitivity and consideration. It's essential to understand that voluntary participation is critical to the success of teamwork, and forcing the issue can lead to resentment and a lack of cooperation.

Furthermore, introducing teamwork to those who may benefit from it must be done in a way that's respectful and tactful. Communication is key, and it's essential to avoid using jargon and buzzwords that can confuse and alienate people.

One area to focus on is collaboration or lack thereof. Collaboration is the process of individuals or groups working together to achieve a common goal or objective. It's a powerful force that can lead to improved performance, increased creativity, and enhanced problem-solving abilities. Collaboration involves sharing ideas, resources, and expertise to achieve a common goal that would be impossible or more challenging to accomplish alone.

One of the main benefits of collaboration is that it fosters a sense of community and shared responsibility. When individuals work together towards a common goal, they feel a sense of ownership and accountability, which leads to higher levels of commitment and motivation. This sense of community also helps to build stronger relationships and fosters a culture of trust and respect.

Collaboration also encourages diversity of thought and perspective, which can lead to more creative and innovative solutions. When individuals with different backgrounds, experiences, and expertise work together, they bring unique ideas and insights to the table, leading to more robust and creative problem-solving.

Furthermore, collaboration can lead to increased productivity and efficiency. When individuals work together, they can divide tasks and responsibilities, allowing each person to focus on their strengths and expertise. This can lead to a more streamlined process and faster completion of tasks.

Finally, collaboration can lead to improved decision-making. When individuals work together, they can share information, insights, and perspectives, leading to more informed and well-rounded decisions. Collaboration also encourages open communication and active listening, which can help to identify potential problems or challenges before they become significant issues.

Collaboration is a powerful force that can lead to improved performance, increased creativity, enhanced problem-solving abilities, stronger relationships, greater efficiency, and better decision-making. By fostering a culture of collaboration, organizations can create a more productive, innovative, and successful workplace.

Another area that can be problematic is when resentment and lack of cooperation settle in. Resentment and a lack of cooperation can arise in a collaborative effort when there is a feeling that someone is being forced to participate or that their contributions are not being valued. It's essential to address these issues promptly to prevent them from escalating and damaging the collaborative effort.

One effective way to overcome resentment and a lack of cooperation is to involve all parties in the decision-making process. When individuals feel that their opinions and contributions are valued, they are more likely to be invested in collaborative efforts. Encouraging open communication and active listening can also help to identify any concerns or issues early on, allowing them to be addressed before they become significant problems.

It's also crucial to ensure that everyone is clear on their roles and responsibilities within the collaborative effort. When individuals understand what is expected of them, they are more likely to feel a sense of ownership and accountability, leading to a greater commitment to the project's success.

Another strategy to overcome resentment and a lack of cooperation is to celebrate successes and milestones throughout the project. Recognizing and acknowledging the contributions of all team members can help to build morale and create a sense of accomplishment, leading to increased motivation and a willingness to continue working collaboratively.

It's important to remember that collaboration is not always easy, and conflicts may arise. When conflicts occur, it's essential to address them promptly and with respect and empathy. Seeking the assistance of a neutral third party, such as a mediator, can also help to resolve conflicts and move the collaborative effort forward.

In summary, overcoming resentment and a lack of cooperation in a collaborative effort requires open communication, active listening, clear roles and responsibilities, recognition of contributions, and prompt resolution of conflicts. By addressing these issues early on and fostering a culture of respect and empathy, organizations can create a more productive and successful collaborative effort.

Finally, it's crucial to remember that teamwork is not a tool for personal gain or to undermine others. It's a collaborative effort that benefits everyone involved. By following these guidelines, you can create a workplace culture that values teamwork and fosters productivity, growth, and success.

7

NOTHING BLUNTS CRITICISM
BETTER THAN SUCCESS

Do you want people to shut up? Just keep winning. Bring people along with you, celebrate individual wins, and recognize your team and peers when you can. All boats rise with the tide. But, when the boat is sinking, it is all men for themselves.

By celebrating and rewarding those who are gunning for you, you can blunt any narrative they might try to create about you. It is hard to overcome success and a win—granted, people try. You just give them another hurdle to get over. Plus, it is a nice poke in the eye when you bring them along and celebrate them in the process.

One way to achieve this is to understand the difference between an activity and an impact. Most people say they are busy but make little to no impact on the overall results or goals. Many people confuse being busy with being productive. Most of the time, they just have poor time management skills or focus on the wrong things. Being in meeting after meeting doesn't make you important or successful. Knowing what meeting to be in and moving the ball forward is being successful.

Hence, you'll hear people complain that they work so hard and don't get any recognition for it. They will say they are busting their butt and then get passed over for a promotion. It is a never-ending stream of excuses. The reality is that they don't focus on the right things and don't achieve any real success. You need to focus on what matters and what is going to make an impact. That will give you the right narrative to share about how you are winning.

Yet sometimes, when you are making a difference and winning, people react in unexpected ways. Once I was yelled at in the breakroom; my general position when being yelled at is to just listen. Don't react. If you have been lucky enough to have worked somewhere where employees are semi-professional people, you will never get a chance to experience some truly remarkable people. And by remarkable, I mean clowns. Working with clowns is a joy and pleasure that I hope you'll never have to experience. Most of the time, it is a circus, and the clowns run the show.

So, going back to being yelled at in the breakroom. True story. I once had a customer service manager yell at me in the breakroom for running a promotion. No kidding. She complained that I was driving up call volume and it was ruining her call center metrics. Seriously. She was more concerned with her call center metrics than driving revenue for the business. The promotion did drive sales, as promotions are supposed to do. Was she unprofessional? Absolutely! Did I respond? No, but I thanked her for everything she did to help our customers. What you see are competing goals. She was more concerned with hold times and dropped calls, which were her metrics, not mine.

What she was really mad about was that she didn't thoughtfully plan for the promotion. She didn't adjust her staffing schedule and didn't do the thing needed to run a call center correctly. She knew the promotion was coming for weeks, and yet there she was, yelling like a fool by the coffee machine. Somehow this was my fault, but most people got a laugh out of it—I know I did.

The key part here is how to react. I didn't. I took the high road because there was no good path forward fighting back. I was winning. The leadership knew what we were doing was right. She made a fool of herself, and I kept winning. You would think that working with adult-aged people would make things more courteous or have grace in their interactions. Disagree. Air opinions. Reach a mutually agreeable solution and go ahead. But you will often run into people who were raised by wolves. Just raw and rude. Have thick skin and do what is right. Never apologize because it just becomes fuel for the fire. Admit when you are wrong, own your mistakes, but an apology should never be found.

Be leery of the folks who say things like, "Nothing personal, just voicing an opinion and trying to make things better." This is usually backhanded double speak to give you a put-down. It's like saying, "with all due respect," and then saying something disrespectful. I think that was in the movie *Talladega Nights*—a classy movie and very applicable here.

But in some companies, terrible behavior and terrible people infest every meeting and every interaction, and it is tolerated. Inexplicably tolerated. I don't know why or how. It just becomes part of the culture. This behavior is also sometimes rewarded, with some terrible people who get promoted. Stir the pot, get a raise. Be useless now that you are now the VP. Crazy! When this usually happens, turnover is typically extremely high. Anyone worth their weight leaves quickly after arriving.

I worked at a large Fintech firm, and nearly 100% of the

marketing turned over within my first year. I had three different managers and went through four reorganizations and layoffs. It was practically the *Hunger Games*! Toxic work environment? It was beyond that, and I was happy to get out of that place. Nothing I could do would have changed the dynamic of that situation. The best choice is to run for the door.

This leads to the concept of "just figure it out." This is the most underrated concept that you should follow. Getting yelled at in the breakroom, just figure it out. Got assigned a new project, just figure it out. Working with a backstabbing succubus, just figure it out. And by figuring it out, you can put yourself on the path toward success. This doesn't mean you have to go at it alone. Bring a team along for the ride, but it also doesn't mean you can't go it alone. Sometimes you just need to figure it out and get it done. I tell my team all the time, "There is not a single thing I ask you to do that I wouldn't or haven't done myself." Yes, I have been the most expensive FedEx envelope stuffer in the building before. Yes, I have opened Illustrator and made edits to a document. Am I a designer? Am I trained in Illustrator? No. But guess what, I figured it out. This kind of success or win is immensely satisfying.

When I worked at one of the Big Four accounting firms, I had a partner say once (actually, he said it all the time), "Plan the work, work the plan." I have heard this saying in other forms and earlier in my career, but it never really stuck with me. But hearing it again, it made sense in terms of how you can set yourself up for success and keep winning. If you think about what needs to be done and plan it out, then work on completing the plan, you have given yourself a roadmap to success. I know this sounds like common sense. And as Mike Tyson famously said, "Everyone has a plan until they get punched in the face."

I like the idea of planning the work part. This blunts any criticism because, in theory, you would share the plan and get buy-in or, at a minimum, cover your butt by telling others what's going on, whether they agree with the plan or not. No surprises. The risk here is being too rigid and not flexible enough when you get punched in the face. How does the plan change or adapt when needed? I never invest too much into a plan, so I can walk away or make changes without saying, "But this is my baby!" If the plan is good, I stick with it, but if it needs to change or be modified in some way or another or killed off completely, then I am okay with that. Sometimes winning means giving up. There is nothing wrong with that. You need to know when to do it and be okay with doing it.

Another concept that you need to embrace for success is the concept of partial solutions. Sometimes a partial solution gets you part of the way to your goal. Sometimes it is easier than trying to drag rocks up a hill to complete the whole project. Other times it is not possible to get 100% of what you want, so a partial win is better than nothing. I have found, at times, that a project will try to do more than it should have. Cutting back on the project to get the win should always be a choice, especially if there is no chance of getting to the end successfully.

The concept of agile development is similar. For those who don't know what agile development is, the basic concept is simple. You take a large software development project and break it up into smaller pieces for short periods or sprints. Get it? You sprint, as in running a short distance. Computer people are so punny. So, the sum of the sprints equals the whole project. These sprints last a few weeks and are iterative. You get quick wins. Your product improves after each sprint, and your customers get to use the features sooner versus waiting months or years for an update. You can easily do this for sales or marketing projects. Makes sense. But just remember, plan the work, work the plan.

A notable example of this concept was a strategic project I was asked to lead. We knew the problem. Customers could not complete the checkout process until we were able to verify income. Typically, that process required having them send us a pay stub. Stop and ask yourself when the last time you saw your pay stub was. With direct deposit, I see the money come in, and the pay stub is a distant afterthought. It might take me a few minutes to remember what online service has it and go find it and download it. This is not an uncommon problem. Nearly twenty-five percent of the orders would need some form of manual verification, and it had an enormous impact on the checkout completion rate. Basically, we had the sale until the system roadblocked it. Here's the great part, though; once I did all that, I had to fax it in to get verified. Just another hurdle and order killer.

Our goal was to eliminate the roadblocks and get more already placed orders to completion, which would, in turn, increase revenue. Simple enough. The challenge here was it was going to be a big project with lots of moving parts, and it could take months or a year, or more to complete the whole thing. Working with our developers and a partner, we decided to break the project up into sprints. Work on one function and then move to the next. This allowed us to quickly get small wins and incremental impacts on revenue. It justified the project and gave us the breathing room to do what we needed to do with less pressure. There were a lot of benefits to focusing on micro-goals. In the end, we saw a double-digit decrease in abandoned orders, which in turn helped us capture revenue that would be easily lost.

My favorite type of meeting is a Blame Storming session or what most folks call a Post-mortem. These meetings serve only one purpose and one purpose only: To find someone or some people to blame. They are never designed to identify the root cause or come up with solutions to prevent the problem from happening again. A post-mortem meeting is a code for finding someone to blame and hiding the real problem. No solutions will be found, but a head on a pike is the name of the game.

Very rarely do these meetings lead to fixing the root cause of the problem. They tend to be uncomfortable events and only contribute to demoralizing employees and creating fear. I have never been in a meeting where the true purpose was to identify and create a solution to prevent a future project from failing the same way. They tend to be grievance fest and a way for others to point fingers away from themselves. Again, sinking ship, the rats will abandon quickly. Any allies quickly turn on you. It is easier to blame people than it is to work to find the right solution to the problem or problems.

Instead, these meetings need to focus on trying to make things better. When I run a postmortem-type meeting, I focus on the problem and not the people. I couldn't care less about the who. I am more concerned about the "why" and how we can prevent this moving forward. I am always forward and future-looking. There is no benefit to finding a boogieman. There is more benefit in finding a path forward. This puts people at ease. Knowing that the witch hunt is about problems, not people.

What to do when you make someone mad? If you are doing your job and whether you are trying to or not, you will make someone mad. It is a simple fact. If you are making people mad, you are unengaged or looking for a new job. Now, you may never know if you are making people mad, but you are.

Every problem has a solution. I want to end this chapter with a solution. Not a solution to any problem you have, but it just seems like the right topic to end this clown show.

But not every person is willing to take the solution.

How do you talk about success when success has silenced criticism? Well, success does that. No one wants to hear the truth, and success is its own proof.

People can't complain when you are getting results, and success has silenced critics.

You are a threat to someone. You always have been. It is human nature. If someone can't compete with you, they are threatened by you.

There is nothing wrong with wanting to be successful. You upset people when you are getting results if they see you as competition; however, you should not care about criticism, and nothing helps silence your critics faster than your success.

Success on a project can be a powerful tool to deflect criticism from others. When a project is completed success-fully, it sends a clear message to everyone involved that the project was well-planned, executed, and delivered as intended. This can help to silence any criticism from those who may have been skeptical or critical of the project's goals, timeline, or budget.

Having a successful project also reinforces the credi-bility of the team and the individuals involved in the project. This can make it more difficult for others to raise valid concerns or objections to future projects, as they will have to consider the successful track record of the team.

Furthermore, a successful project can also demonstrate the effectiveness of the processes and tools used in the project, making it easier to argue in favor of similar approaches in the future.

Another factor that can help to blunt criticism is the sense of pride and ownership that comes with a successful project. When people have worked hard on a project and seen it come to fruition, they are naturally more invested in it and less likely to be critical of it. This sense of pride can help to foster a positive and supportive team culture, where members are less likely to be critical of one another's work and more likely to offer constructive feedback.

Finally, having a successful project can help to establish a positive reputation for the individuals and the team. This can be particularly important for those who are looking to advance their careers or gain recognition for their work. Having a successful project on their portfolio can demonstrate their ability to deliver quality work and help them to stand out from the crowd.

In conclusion, success on a project can play a critical role in blunting criticism from others. By demonstrating the effectiveness of the team and the processes used, fostering a positive team culture, and establishing a positive reputation, success can help to deflect any negative feedback and create a more supportive environment for future projects.

8

SHINY OBJECT SYNDROME (S.O.S.)

Don't let perfect get in the way of better. 80% of something is better than 100% of nothing. Focus is hard to sustain. Most people want to be on the new and exciting projects and easily give up on the current projects or tasks. I like to call this S.O.S. or shiny object syndrome.

In today's fast-paced work environment, it's easy to get caught up in the excitement of new projects and tasks. However, constantly shifting from one thing to another can hinder productivity and make it difficult to accomplish anything. S.O.S. can be particularly problematic for people who are easily distracted or struggle with maintaining focus.

One way to combat S.O.S. is to limit distractions as much as possible. This means setting aside specific times during the day to check email, social media, and other non-work-related tasks. By doing this, you'll be able to stay focused on the project at hand without getting sidetracked by notifications or other distractions.

Another important factor in staying focused is setting clear goals for each project or task. This means breaking down larger goals into smaller, more manageable tasks and then setting deadlines for each one. By doing this, you'll be able to track your progress and stay motivated, even when the work feels challenging.

Ultimately, it's important to remember that sometimes 80% of something is better than 100% of nothing. While it's always important to strive for excellence, there are times when it's better to focus on completing tasks to the best of your ability rather than getting bogged down in perfectionism. By staying focused, limiting distractions, and setting clear goals, you'll be able to accomplish more and feel more satisfied with your work.

In the beginning, it is easy to focus on one project or task, but as you get into it, more and more of your focus will shift towards something you haven't even started yet. This can be a dangerous path to go down since there will always be a shiny object off in the distance beckoning you with its siren song. Most organizations and departments struggle with this issue. It is why some projects never seem to end or have constant leadership changes, hoping for different outcomes.

The grass is not always greener on the other side. Again, sometimes 80% of something is better than 100% of nothing. Yes, that means sometimes 20% of a project might not be bad either. If you lose focus on 100%, then I imagine that might result in 80%. Maybe just focus on the tasks at hand and see what happens. But this is hard for most organizations to do.

I think it is important to understand the 80/20 rule, also known as the Pareto concept. The Pareto concept, also known as the Pareto principle or the 80/20 rule, states that roughly 80% of effects come from 20% of causes. This principle can be applied to a variety of situations, including work productivity and project management.

In the context of work productivity, the Pareto concept suggests that roughly 80% of results come from 20% of effort. This means that it's important to focus on the tasks and projects that will yield the greatest results rather than getting bogged down in smaller, less impactful tasks.

The 80/20 rule can also be applied to project management. In this context, it suggests that 80% of a project's results come from 20% of the project's tasks. This means that it's important to identify the most critical tasks and focus on completing them first rather than getting side-tracked by less important tasks.

By applying the 80/20 rule to work productivity and project management, you can increase your efficiency and effectiveness. By focusing on the tasks that will yield the greatest results and prioritizing them accordingly, you'll be able to accomplish more in less time and with less effort. This, in turn, can lead to greater job satisfaction and a sense of accomplishment.

Another way to look at this is my focus equation: focus + focus = focus. No, that doesn't equal zero; it equals focus! Just keep an eye out for the shiny object in the corner of your eye. It is there but not worth losing focus over, or maybe it gets a priority later, or another team gets to work on it.

Another concept I have been exposed to is from the United States Marine Corps. The US Marines' 70%-rule is a concept that suggests that in situations where you don't have all the information or resources needed to make a decision, it's better to decide with 70% of the information than to wait for more information and risk missing an opportunity.

In the context of work productivity and project management, the 70%-rule can be applied in a few different ways. For example, if you're working on a project and you're not sure whether to proceed with a particular task or not, the 70%-rule suggests that it's better to decide with the information you have, rather than waiting for more information and potentially missing a deadline.

Similarly, if you're managing a team and you're not sure whether to delegate a particular task to a team member or to handle it yourself, the 70%-rule suggests that it's better to delegate the task with the information you have, rather than hold onto it and potentially miss out on the opportunity to focus on more critical tasks.

In the context of the Pareto concept, the 70%-rule can help you prioritize tasks and make decisions that will maximize your productivity and effectiveness. By focusing on the tasks that will yield the greatest results and making decisions with the information you have, rather than waiting for perfect information or conditions, you'll be able to accomplish more in less time and with greater efficiency.

The 70%-rule can be a useful tool in increasing productivity and efficiency in project management because it encourages decision-making and action-taking in situations where the optimal path is not immediately clear. When faced with uncertainty or incomplete information, waiting for perfect conditions or additional information can cause delays and lead to missed opportunities. The 70%-rule suggests that it is better to make a decision with incomplete information rather than waiting for perfect conditions.

In project management, the 70%-rule can help prioritize tasks and prevent unnecessary delays. For example, if a task is essential to the project's success but requires additional information or resources, it may be better to proceed with what is currently available and revisit the task later as additional information becomes available. This can prevent delays and ensure progress is made on other tasks that can be completed with the available information.

Additionally, the 70%-rule can help with delegation and decision-making. When managing a team, a leader can use the 70%-rule to delegate tasks to team members who have the necessary information or resources to complete a task with incomplete information. This not only helps in getting the task done but also empowers team members to make decisions and act.

The 70%-rule is a valuable tool for increasing productivity and efficiency in project management. Encouraging decision-making and action-taking in situations where complete information is not available can help prevent unnecessary delays, prioritize tasks, and empower team members to make decisions and act.

While both the 80/20 rule and the 70%-rule are productivity concepts, there are some key differences between the two.

The 80/20 rule suggests that roughly 80% of effects come from 20% of causes. In the context of work productivity and project management, the 80/20 rule suggests that roughly 80% of a project's results come from 20% of the project's tasks. The primary benefit of the 80/20 rule is that it helps prioritize tasks and prevents wasting time on low-impact tasks. However, the downside is that it can also lead to neglecting important but lower-impact tasks, which can have long-term negative consequences.

On the other hand, the 70%-rule suggests that in situations where you don't have all the information or resources needed to make a decision, it's better to decide with 70% of the information than to wait for more information and risk missing an opportunity. The primary benefit of the 70%-rule is that it encourages action-taking and decision-making in situations of uncertainty, preventing delays and missed opportunities. However, the downside is that it can also lead to making suboptimal decisions due to incomplete information or lack of resources.

So, the 80/20 rule is primarily focused on prioritizing tasks and maximizing efficiency, while the 70%-rule is focused on acting and making decisions in situations of uncertainty. Both concepts have their pros and cons, and understanding the nuances of each can help in determining which is most appropriate in a given situation.

Here are some of the pros of the 80/20 rule.

- It helps prioritize tasks and prevent wasting time on low-impact tasks.
- It increases efficiency by focusing on high-impact tasks.
- It can lead to faster completion of projects and tasks.
- It provides a framework for decision-making and resource allocation.
- It helps identify areas for improvement and optimization.
- It encourages a focus on results rather than just effort.
- It can be applied in various contexts, from personal productivity to business strategy.
- It can help maximize return on investment (ROI) by focusing on the most profitable customers or products.

THESE ARE JUST a few of the benefits of applying the 80/20 rule in your work and personal life. By focusing on the tasks and activities that have the greatest impact, you can increase your efficiency and productivity and achieve better results in less time.

In comparison, here are some of the pros of the 70%-rule.

- It encourages action-taking and decision-making in situations of uncertainty.
- It helps prevent delays and missed opportunities.
- It empowers individuals and teams to make decisions with incomplete information.
- It provides a framework for managing risk.
- It can lead to more agile and responsive decision-making.
- It encourages experimentation and innovation.
- It can help build confidence and resilience in decision-making.
- It helps identify areas where additional information or resources are needed.

THESE ARE JUST a few of the benefits of applying the 70%-rule in your work and personal life. By making decisions with incomplete information and acting in situations of uncertainty, you can increase your agility and responsiveness and make progress even in the face of uncertainty.

So, let me ask you this question: How much focus do you have right now? I bet you have a million things to do, and all of them are a priority. But what are the ones that need to get done, and which ones will have the most impact on your business?

My advice is to focus on what is most important and never lose focus on the tasks at hand, and don't become a victim of S.O.S. Here are some suggestions I use to keep the focus:

1. Get in the habit of finishing projects.
2. Recognize focus as a precious resource.
3. Keep track of upcoming deadlines.
4. Utilize focus groups.
5. Don't be work-obsessed.
6. Schedule downtime.
7. Recognize focus shifts.
8. Avoid multitasking.
9. Minimize distractions.
10. Limit interruptions.
11. Set limits on focus time.
12. Set realistic focus goals.
13. Don't expect perfection.
14. Distinguish between good and bad multitasking.
15. Stop chasing the next new thing or project.
16. Stay focused in conversation.
17. Maintain focus during meetings.
18. Quit trying to be perfect.
19. Don't let your day get away from you, and get organized.
20. Accept that some things will never get done.
21. Avoid being too hard on yourself.
22. Be fully present.
23. Know when to quit.

24. Make time for fun.
25. Identify and stop procrastination.

I HOPE these focus suggestions help you get back to focusing on what is at hand and staying focused. I have even heard that some people have a separate "parking lot" just for shiny objects so they can keep up with them and get focused on them when the time is right. This can help you stay focused while keeping an eye out for special opportunities when they arise.

In this chapter, we discussed various productivity concepts, including the Pareto principle (the 80/20 rule) and the 70%-rule. We explored how these concepts can be applied in work productivity and project management and their respective pros and cons. The 80/20 rule is beneficial in prioritizing tasks, increasing efficiency, and achieving better results in less time, while the 70%-rule is useful in making decisions and taking action in situations of uncertainty, preventing delays and missed opportunities, and building confidence in decision-making. Overall, understanding and applying these productivity concepts can help individuals and teams optimize their productivity and effectiveness.

Remember that focus is key, whether it is the 70%-rule or the 80/20 rule, focusing on 80% or the 70% of something is always better than focusing on 100% of nothing. So, get back to working on your project and the tasks at hand instead of being distracted by the shiny object in the corner.

9

NO TIME LIKE THE PRESENT TO FOCUS!

You know that feeling when you're so caught up in a project, and it's going well, but then the urge to move on to something new starts creeping in? Then you start thinking, this is making me happy now, but I'm not sure what will happen next. What if I get bored? That's how we feel all the time—constantly chasing our tails with only an idea of where they might lead us. We live for novelty and excitement at work because it feels good while we're doing it. But eventually, those highs become lows as life becomes monotonous again without any semblance of what comes next. It's hard to stay focused on one thing long enough to see its endgame or reap its benefits.

In the words of the late Steve Jobs, "Focus is about saying, 'No.'" It can be so easy to get distracted with new projects and start chasing shiny objects when you should just focus on what matters most now. The good news is that there are a few simple ways for you to limit your distractions and stay focused on what needs to happen right now to achieve your long-term goals. Here are some ideas for how you can avoid being pulled into distracting tasks by focusing on today's priorities instead:

- Turn off notifications from social media apps like Facebook Messenger or Instagram if they distract you too much during work hours.
- Have designated times when you check emails (try setting different time intervals throughout the day).

TOO OFTEN, we are so concerned with chasing after new initiatives that have yet to be proven successful or even tried before, while neglecting our current priorities and leaving us unprepared for what is happening in front of us today. To avoid this trap, focus your attention on where you need it most—on the things within your control now—and stop worrying about all those other shiny objects out there. You can't do them justice if they're not a top priority at the moment.

So how do you focus on the important tasks while avoiding the dangers of multitasking? Here are some strategies to help focus at work:

- Create a priority list for your projects and focus on finishing each task in order.
- Don't start working on something new until you're finished with the last thing you started.

- Reward yourself when you complete an important task or finish one step in your project, no matter how small it might seem at the time.
- Shut off distractions. Close social media sites, put your phone on silent and turn off email alerts.

DON'T ALLOW yourself to get distracted by nonvital jobs that don't impact major milestones. By learning to focus on work, you will be able to focus on the important tasks when they are required.

Stay organized and keep a to-do list going and prioritize the things that need to be done first. When you finish one task, check it off your list and focus your attention on the next one.

Limit distractions by turning off all notifications for email and other applications. Focus can also be broken down into smaller chunks of time by creating a schedule where you focus only on specific things from 8-11 am or 1-4 pm every day. If something is not critical, don't even open those emails, as this will help avoid unnecessary distractions every day. By scheduling focus, you force yourself to let go of distractions, as the focus can only be broken by a set time.

Don't focus on trying to complete a task until it is 100% perfect. Nothing is ever going to be 100%, and the effort to get it there is nearly impossible. If you're not going to focus properly, it will negatively impact your other tasks and may even lead to multiple mistakes or errors throughout your work, which can be hard to catch up with if things are missed early on. Completing everything won't necessarily make you look better, as there's no way of telling what will be looked upon more favorably. Don't let perfection get in the way of progress.

To focus effectively, clear out distractions from your workspace and focus only on one job at a time without switching between different tasks because once you switch focus, it takes a while for your mind to get back into focus.

If there are things that you need to focus on and focus on for a long time, it may be best to do these away from your workspace where there are fewer distractions. Instead, focus at home or somewhere with fewer distractions so that you can focus effectively and work toward your goals without interruption.

There is never enough time in the day, but we make sure we focus as much as possible every day because we know what matters most—family, health, and achieving life's purpose. Having just one focused hour per day will give you more than enough power you need for the rest of the day. You just need to start focusing now and not let distractions stop you anymore.

Don't focus on multitasking or focus on trying to complete multiple things at once because this will only give mixed results and might not be the best choice for certain tasks. Instead, focus your attention on one task at a time which means that you should take care of what's most important now instead of taking care of everything. Multitasking is a fallacy.

Focus is key when it comes down to completing projects successfully, as well as enjoying life more by reducing stress levels, anxiety issues, and other problems affecting the mind. If you want to focus on your life, make sure to set priorities and focus on those first before anything else—including other people's opinions or complaints about how they think something should be done. It isn't your problem until it becomes your problem, so focus on what you can focus on now. Make sure to focus your energy on the things that matter most instead of the things that don't. Focus on everything with integrity and not just because it is convenient or makes you look better for completing everything.

It's easy to fixate on deadlines, but this often means missing out on life itself, which is why focus might need to be broken down into smaller chunks of time. For example, create a schedule where you focus only on specific things from 8-11 am or 1-4 pm every day.

After doing work, make sure to take some time off and relax before focusing again because once focus is broken, it takes a while for your mind to go back into focus mode. If you focus too much, you'll end up with burnout which can cause more harm than good.

If focus is something that you struggle with every day due to distractions or even laziness (when the focus turns into procrastination), then it may be time for you to focus on your personal life again.

Find out how to focus without being stressed by making focus intentional instead of unintentional. That way, you can focus on what matters most in your life regardless of if things go right or wrong. If focus is broken, make sure to figure out where the problem occurs so you can start focusing better no matter what distractions come your way. There's always a solution when it comes down to maintaining focus at work and concentrating on important tasks.

Just don't get distracted by the shiny objects. Stay focused on what is strategic, what is important, and what moves the needle to help you reach your goals. But equally important, do not forget to focus on yourself, your family, your friends, and other things besides work.

As human beings, it's natural for us to seek out novelty

and excitement in our lives. We crave the rush of starting something new and making progress toward a goal, but the reality is that this pursuit of constant novelty can often lead us astray from our long-term objectives.

When we become too focused on the thrill of a new project or idea, we can easily lose sight of our current priorities and responsibilities. It's crucial to strike a balance between exploring new opportunities and staying focused on the present.

As Steve Jobs famously said, "Focus is about saying, 'No.'" This means that we must learn to say no to distractions and shiny objects that don't align with our current priorities. It's important to prioritize our time and energy on the things that matter most right now rather than constantly chasing after the next big thing.

One way to avoid getting sidetracked is by turning off notifications from social media apps and other distractions during work hours. Another effective strategy is to set designated times to check emails and messages, such as once every hour or twice a day. This can help you stay focused on your tasks and avoid getting sidetracked by incoming messages or getting pulled into unrelated tasks.

Ultimately, it's important to remember that success is a marathon, not a sprint. By focusing on your current priorities and avoiding distractions, you'll be better equipped to achieve your long-term goals and enjoy sustained success. So the next time you feel the urge to chase after a shiny object, take a step back and remind yourself of what truly matters at that moment.

In addition to limiting distractions and staying focused on your current priorities, it's important to cultivate a growth mindset. This means embracing challenges and failures as opportunities for growth and learning. When we are too focused on perfection or immediate success, we can easily get discouraged and lose sight of our goals.

By embracing a growth mindset, we can learn from our mistakes and setbacks and use them as stepping stones toward achieving our long-term objectives. This also helps us develop resilience and adaptability, two critical skills for success in today's fast-paced and ever-changing world.

Another way to stay focused on your goals is by breaking them down into smaller, manageable tasks. This can help make your goals feel more achievable and less overwhelming. By setting specific, measurable, and time-bound objectives, you can stay motivated and track your progress toward your long-term goals.

It's also important to remember that success is not just about achieving your goals but also about maintaining your momentum and staying committed to your vision over the long term. This requires discipline, perseverance, and a willingness to adapt and evolve as circumstances change.

Staying focused on your priorities and avoiding distractions is critical for achieving success in both your personal and professional life. By cultivating a growth mindset, breaking down your goals into manageable tasks, and staying committed to your vision, you can achieve sustained success and enjoy a fulfilling and rewarding life.

Limiting distractions is crucial for staying focused on your goals and achieving success. In today's world, we are constantly bombarded with notifications, messages, and other distractions that can easily pull us away from our priorities and tasks.

It's also important to create a work environment that supports focus and productivity. This may mean finding a quiet workspace, using noise-canceling headphones, or setting up boundaries with coworkers or family members to limit interruptions during work hours.

Finally, it's important to be mindful of your own habits and tendencies when it comes to distractions. Are there certain apps or websites that tend to distract you more than others? Are there certain times of day when you are more prone to getting sidetracked? By being aware of your patterns and tendencies, you can take steps to limit distractions and stay focused on your priorities.

Limiting distractions is a critical component of staying focused and achieving success. By turning off notifications, setting designated times for checking emails, creating a supportive work environment, and being mindful of your habits and tendencies, you can avoid getting sidetracked and stay on track toward your goals.

Focusing on priorities is essential for achieving success and making progress toward your long-term goals. Here are some steps you can take to help you stay focused on your priorities:

1. **Define your priorities**: Before you can focus on your priorities, you need to know what they are. Take some time to identify your key goals and objectives, both short-term and long-term. Write them down and prioritize them in order of importance.

2. **Break down your goals into smaller tasks**: Once you have identified your priorities, it can be helpful to break them down into smaller, more manageable tasks. This can help you stay focused and avoid feeling overwhelmed. Set specific,

measurable, and time-bound objectives for each
task, and track your progress as you work
towards your goals.

3. **Create a schedule**: Having a schedule can help
you stay on track and avoid getting sidetracked by
other tasks or distractions. Set aside dedicated
time for your most important tasks and block out
time for focused work without interruptions.
This can help you stay focused and make progress
toward your priorities.

4. **Learn to say "No"**: Saying no to non-essential
tasks or requests can be difficult, but it is essential
for staying focused on your priorities. Be clear
about your priorities and commitments, and learn
to say "No" to tasks that do not align with your
goals or take up too much time.

5. **Eliminate distractions**: As mentioned earlier,
distractions can be a major obstacle to staying
focused on your priorities. Take steps to eliminate
distractions, such as turning off notifications,
finding a quiet workspace, or using noise-
canceling headphones.

6. **Stay motivated**: Staying motivated and
committed to your priorities can be challenging,
especially when faced with setbacks or obstacles.
Find ways to stay motivated, such as visualizing
your goals, tracking your progress, or rewarding
yourself for achieving milestones.

FOCUSING on your priorities requires a combination of
discipline, organization, and motivation. By defining your
priorities, breaking them down into smaller tasks, creating

a schedule, learning to say no, eliminating distractions, and staying motivated, you can stay focused and make progress towards your goals.

Timeboxing is a time management technique that involves dividing your workday into dedicated periods, or "boxes," for specific tasks or activities. During each time box, you focus solely on the designated task without interruptions or distractions.

The idea behind timeboxing is that by setting specific, dedicated periods of time for each task, you can increase your focus, productivity, and efficiency. By eliminating distractions and interruptions, you can stay in a state of flow and make progress toward your goals.

Timeboxing can benefit your focus in several ways:

- **Improved focus and concentration**: When you dedicate a specific block of time to a task, you eliminate the distractions that can pull you away from your work. By focusing solely on the task at hand during the time box, you can increase your focus and concentration and make progress toward your goals.
- **Increased productivity and efficiency**: By setting specific time limits for each task, you can increase your productivity and efficiency. You are forced to work within a specific time frame, which can help you prioritize your work and avoid getting sidetracked by non-essential tasks.
- **Reduced procrastination**: Timeboxing can help reduce procrastination by breaking down large or daunting tasks into smaller, more manageable

time boxes. By setting specific goals for each time box, you can make progress towards your goals and feel a sense of accomplishment, which can help reduce procrastination and increase motivation.

- **Improved time management**: By planning out your day in advance and allocating specific timeboxes for each task, you can improve your time management skills. You can prioritize your most important tasks and make the most of your time without getting sidetracked by non-essential tasks or distractions.

TIMEBOXING IS a time management technique that involves dividing your workday into dedicated time periods for specific tasks or activities. By eliminating distractions, increasing focus and concentration, and improving productivity and efficiency, timeboxing can help you stay focused and achieve your goals.

This chapter focused on the importance of staying focused on priorities to achieve success. It discussed the natural human tendency to crave novelty and excitement but also the importance of saying, "No" to distractions and shiny objects that do not align with our goals. The chapter then went on to describe several strategies for limiting distractions, such as turning off notifications and setting designated times for checking emails. It also emphasized the importance of cultivating a growth mindset, breaking down goals into manageable tasks, and staying committed to your vision. The chapter concluded with a discussion of the benefits of timeboxing, a time management technique that involves dividing your workday into dedicated time periods for specific tasks or activities. The overall message of the chapter is that by staying focused on priorities, eliminating distractions, and managing your time effectively, you can achieve success and fulfillment in both your personal and professional life.

10

PO-PO VS. HI-PO

I never started out wanting to be a change management professional, but it ended up being one of the things that I have had to do regularly to help my teams get through organizational changes. In the past year, I have had to help my team through a lot of changes, and they stepped up to the task every time. But why? How did I do it?

The employees who are the biggest assets in my company are the ones who will help me through changes. It's not just because they want to get through change, but it is because they can't thrive when things go wrong. They enjoy the challenge, and it helps our customers and helps us move forward as an organization.

I also found that some employees benefited from meeting one-on-one with me regularly as part of their performance management before any organizational changes happened.

What you need to do with your high-performing employees is to allow them to take more risks than others within the organization. These employees love challenges and opportunities where they can use their intelligence and creativity. This helps employees understand why there are changes and how those changes are setting them up for something new. However, don't give these employees too much change in the initial phases because it would be out of their comfort zones, and they may feel overwhelmed or afraid.

One way I managed employees when changes were happening was by not giving them all the information upfront. This led employees to ask more questions, which was great for me. It allowed conversations to open up about what was happening in the organization. Then I could help employees learn about the changes as we went along and break the status quo and find new ways of doing things.

High-performing (Hi-Po) employees can be found at all levels of employees, too, so don't assume that high-performance employees only come from management or upper management ranks. They are the employees who get things done, get them done well, and get them done on time. They're employees who will go above and beyond their job duties to help the organization succeed without being asked.

In addition, employees who have a high level of performance empower other employees because these employees model positive behavior that other employees emulate. Change management professionals need to give Hi-Po employees opportunities to showcase what they can do when there is pressure to perform, provide clear direction, allow questions, don't give up if results are not immediate, and take their time in figuring out how changes will work—it's an overall process.

I've already introduced Hi-Po, but what about Po-Po? Never heard of a Po-Po? But I bet you have seen one. Po-Po stands for Passed Over and Pissed Off.

I've been an employee at my company for over ten years now. I have always felt that I have done my best work and worked hard to further the company's goals. Recently, my boss announced promotion opportunities for employees who had gone above and beyond what was expected of them, with the number one promotion going to someone with half as much experience as me. It seems unfair.

What would you say?

You might be tempted to tell your employee that it's perfectly understandable that they are upset because they were passed over for less experienced candidates. While it may be tempting to gloss over their feelings completely, remember that not everyone handles disappointment well. So instead of ignoring what happened altogether, you should acknowledge their feelings.

Offer empathy by trying to put yourself in their shoes. For example, say something like, "I can see why you're upset after not receiving this promotion. I can understand how it would make you feel like you've been left behind." Even if the promotion wasn't what your employee wanted, chances are they applied for it because they felt ready, and getting a promotion is important to them.

Validate what your employee's contributions have been over the years. You don't have to downplay the promotion that was given out but explain how hard it is to decide who gets promoted when there are so many great employees needing recognition.

While avoiding promotion opportunities may seem disrespectful, try not to take it personally and remember those promotion decisions are not always popular. Also, don't be afraid to ask your employees for feedback and suggestions on how you can communicate promotion criteria better in the future.

The key here is to recognize the Po-Po employees and have a plan to deal with them. Focus on why they are where they are and support your plan of attack with data.

This will show that you are genuinely interested in making them feel heard and not just mad or disappointed.

In the end, promotion decisions are based on a variety of factors from education to experience but remember those reasons may be personal as well as professional. If you need some help explaining promotion criteria better to your employees, work with your human resources team, who can do it for you.

If this promotion was about overall performance instead of hard work and overall contribution, make sure your employee is aware they still have a chance at promotion if they continue to perform at their current level. Let them know promotions can happen at any time, so don't get discouraged despite their disappointment.

The harder conversions need to occur when someone is not moving up; instead, they need to be moved out. I have always operated under the belief of Up or Out. If you are just going to stay Po-Po and not do yourself any favors to change your situation, I want to bring in someone who will.

So, while it is important to encourage and coach someone to their potential, it is equally important to know the right time to cut bait and move on to a better resource. Po-Po's can bring down the team morale and hinder its performance. You just need to be aware of these types of situations and act at the appropriate time. Act too quickly, and you may be throwing diamonds in the rough away, but act too late, and you risk poisoning the team.

But how do you go about identifying a high-potential or high-performing employee? It might seem easy. They do their job and do it well. But that is not always the right answer because I have seen plenty of hard workers who never develop to their potential.

As businesses strive to maintain a competitive edge, they are increasingly focused on identifying and developing high-potential employees. These are the employees who have the potential to make a significant impact on the business and who can be groomed for leadership positions.

There are several ways to identify high-potential employees. One is to look at their performance relative to others in their role. Another is to look at their ability to take on new challenges and responsibilities. And finally, their potential can be assessed through psychometric tests and other assessment tools.

Once high-potential employees have been identified, it is important to develop them so that they can reach their full potential. This can be done through mentorship programs, training and development opportunities, and stretch assignments. By investing in the development of high-potential employees, businesses can ensure that they have a pipeline of leaders who are prepared to take the business to the next level. It is as much about training as it is about hands-on coaching.

You will need to invest in them. And as with most investments, there is no guarantee that the investment will pay off. Time and money—the more valuable being your time.

You must spend time with them. Getting to know them, their goals and motivations. What drives them?

Be available to answer their questions, help them solve problems, and give guidance when needed but also step back when they don't need you anymore.

This is not a one-time event; it's an ongoing relationship that should be nurtured over time.

It's important to remember that not every high-potential employee will become a leader in your company. But by investing in the development of these employees, you will improve your chances of finding the next generation of leaders for your business.

But what do you do with employees who think they are high-performing but are not? This is challenging because there is a mismatch between what they think and how they perform.

The first step is acknowledging that there is a problem. This can be difficult for managers because they may not want to upset the employee or make them feel like they are not valued. However, it is important to have a conversation with the employee to discuss the issue. During this conversation, it is important to be clear about what the expectations are and where the employee needs to improve. It is also important to provide feedback in a way that is constructive and helpful.

Once the problem has been identified, the next step is to come up with a plan to address it. This plan should be designed to help the employee improve their performance. It should be specific and measurable so that it is easy to track progress. Additionally, the plan should be realistic and achievable so that the employee does not become discouraged.

The final step is to implement the plan and provide support to the employee. This may include additional training or coaching. It is important to follow up with the employee regularly to ensure that they are making progress. If the employee is not improving, then it may be necessary to take additional actions, such as reassigning tasks or changing roles.

Managing unhappy employees can be challenging, but it

is important to do so to maintain a high-performing team. By taking the time to identify the problem, develop a plan, and provide support, you can help your employees be successful and improve their overall satisfaction.

Again, the challenge is bursting their bubble, but if you have the right conversation and then move to a plan to get them on track, it won't be too difficult. You do have to know going in that they might end up leaving, and that is okay. I'd rather have a bad employee leave than have them stay and poison the team. Never use the excuse, "I don't want to lose the headcount." I call BS, and you are doing yourself a disservice. It is okay to let bad employees leave.

11

NETWORKING IS IMPORTANT

Don't be annoying about it. Hint: LinkedIn isn't some magical networking honeypot, and if your whole networking strategy is based on LinkedIn, you're an idiot. So what to do?

The one thing most people do not do or do extremely poorly is networking. Further, people do not realize that there are only two types of networking—internal and external. Granted, maybe people know about internal and external networking, but people do not do either well or outright just ignore internal networking altogether.

Why only connect with someone when you need something?

How shallow and how presumptuous of you to think I am going to go out of my way to help you when we never talk: "Of course, I'll help you since I haven't heard from you in a year. Your name is Steve, right? Or is it, Bob?"

Stop selling and start connecting. What do you think is the expected outcome of this type of networking?

If you only network or reach out when you need something, nothing will come of the effort. I'll help anyone, but your level of effort must match your engagement. If we chat every few months and exchange emails now and then, I will probably go out of my way to help however I can, even if I don't like it all that much.

Flipside, if I haven't heard from you in months or even years and your email starts with, "long time no talk," your chance of getting my full attention is small. Your effort needs to match the ask. I can't count the number of times when people did not hide their feelings for me (i.e., they didn't like me) but got affected at work, and suddenly they needed my help. It is the equivalent of going on a first date, never calling or texting or emailing back for a year, and then sending me a note asking if I want to start dating. Where have you been? Not going to get anywhere. The same goes for networking.

When it comes to offering recommendations or connecting you with someone about a job, it is my reputation that is on the line, not yours. If you are not engaging with me regularly—and I don't mean daily or weekly, but often enough for me to remember what you look like without going on LinkedIn—I am not willing to risk my goodwill with my contacts to help you. I need to see that the street is moving in both directions. Without that, you come across as selfish and someone who only wants to connect when you need something.

Now, am I guilty of this? Absolutely. Have I reached out to people knowing full well I haven't talked to them in ages? Yes, I have. Did I do that for selfish reasons? Yes, yes, I did. But did I just say the opposite a few paragraphs back? Yep. Go back to my earlier statement; there will be contradictions.

To be candid, I did it because I was afraid. Losing a job or needing to change my work situation forced me (and most people) to panic. What am I going to do? How do I pay my bills? So, when you are afraid, you flail. When you flail, you do something stupid. In this case, reaching out to people I knew very well couldn't and/or wouldn't help me was a way for me to feel like I was trying to do something, and it superficially made me feel better.

But once you stop being afraid and take a deep breath, you go back to your network and do it the right way. If you have made an effort to keep in touch with key people, people who can and will help you when asked, you realize your situation is only temporary. In every job or transition I have had, my network was key to helping me find the right path to a new opportunity.

In almost every case, I ended up in a better place and with more money. This is quite different from me blasting out emails to everyone screaming in desperation—HELP ME!?!?!

With that, stop messing up LinkedIn. You need to consider this when you think about networking. Collecting LinkedIn contacts is not the way to go. Connecting with everyone and anything is not the way to go. When I see someone with 25,000 contacts or, even worse, seeing it written in their profile with them bragging about the number of connections they have, it makes me cringe. I mean, seriously, what is the point? It is not like the number of connections you have on a social network matters to anyone except to you or people like you—those who have the same goals.

To be real, 99% of those so-called 25,000 contacts won't and cannot help you because they are not real. They are superficial at best. Random LinkedIn requests are pointless. Now I am not saying don't connect with people you don't know; I am saying have a plan on what you will do with that contact.

Collecting connections is a big red flag. LinkedIn LION? Seriously, what is that? What is the point? You don't know me, and I don't know you. How can we seriously help each other? In what meaningful way is this a good thing?

In the past, I have seen the mutual connections listed on someone's profile and reached out to my connection only to get a response back, "Oh, I really don't know him." Huh? Can you explain to me how this connection is a good connection? You can't.

Granted, most LinkedIn users just connect to try to sell you something or to build their LinkedIn connection horde. They think this approach is effective, but they are just lazy salespeople or trying to be a LinkedIn LION—again, I don't even know what that means. I can sniff out a sales related LinkedIn request from a mile away. These get ignored.

There is no good outcome for collecting LinkedIn connections. But LinkedIn can be effective when used together with real networking. It also helps open the doors to other potential connections. It is easy to start a conversation with someone you do not know by saying, "We have mutual professional connections. I'd love to connect and figure out how we can help each other."

If I meet you in person, at a meeting or event, I tend to gravitate toward using LinkedIn to connect. It is an effortless way to send a reminder and say it was nice meeting you today. Let's connect. Let's grab lunch or coffee. Let's see how we can help each other. Follow up on the conversation you just had. It is easy.

When I have mentored or coached someone, at some point in the conversation, the networking question always arises. Mostly around these questions:

"What events should I attend?"

"What professional associations should I join?"

"Should I be more active on LinkedIn?"

I WANT TO SAY, "Great short questions," but I don't. I should, but I don't. I do think that these are good questions, but they are a small part of a bigger task you need to tackle. These are activities and not a networking strategy. You need to ask yourself, how does doing these things help me in the bigger picture?

They don't help when done in isolation or in the context of not being part of a bigger personal networking plan. Don't get me wrong, an external event, such as a tradeshow or speaking series, is a wonderful opportunity to network. Hell, I have gotten a lot of business and found many vendors at such events. But it shouldn't be the only thing you do, and there is no magic bullet.

These types of events aren't always a sea of milk and honey. Once, I was at an event and felt like the one hooker with all my teeth. Sales guy after sales guy. Quite popular, but I was there to buy or find a new vendor. Being constantly hammered and given the same speech about how what they do is so much better than the guy you just spoke to. It becomes a turn-off. Because you must remember that people are attending these events with the same or more aggressive goals than you, and they probably don't have a plan besides giving a business card to anything that remotely breathes.

While these proactive external activities are important, sometimes some of the best networking is in your own office. Yes, attend events, join groups that interest you or groups that focus on skills you want to improve and use LinkedIn—the right way. For the love of God, stop messing up LinkedIn, and don't forget to look at internal networking.

Finally, stop posting inspirational crap unless you create it. One, everyone is doing it, and two, everyone is doing it. Be different.

Here are ten things that require zero talent:

1. Reposting ten things that require zero talent on LinkedIn.

I GET you are moved by it, but is it professional? Come up with your own quote. Make a statement about your thought process or how you overcome challenges. Reposting someone else's crap diminishes your credibility.

The Michael Jordan quote just needs to go away, and the fact you posted it doesn't make you more likable or make me want to connect with you. All you end up with is people like you, and it completely defeats the purpose of LinkedIn. You want to connect with people not like you so you can learn and grow.

Try to be unique and creative and be a source of inspiration to others. Being a lemming and reposting another person's work/creativity is lazy.

Oh, and post one of those stupid math problems that only a genius can solve, and I unfollow you at once.

Internal networking is the networking you are not doing. If you work for a larger company that may have multiple offices across the country or the world, you have an even bigger networking opportunity. This provides big opportunities for you to network, not only for the future—for future jobs or to get a mentor, or get help with coaching on how to get to the next level of your career.

Not once in all the conversations I have had, did the person ask about internal networking. When I mention it, I get a blank stare and then an "Oh."

You might be asking yourself, what are the benefits of networking internally? Surprisingly, it has less to do with your current job than you think. Although, some benefits could help you with your current role. But the big benefit of networking internally is your next job or role, whether that is with the same company or with a new company.

People leave jobs all the time, and getting to know someone and connecting with them so they get to know you is important. More important than you might think.

Let's take a few examples. The first one comes from early in my career and how it is affecting me now. I had just started to work for the phone company (and yes, that makes me sound old). But I worked on the internet side of the phone company. I worked on the team that sent out CDs to get people to sign up for dial-up internet service. Ok, that does make me sound old.

Anyway. I started to think about what I wanted to do and where the company was spending resources—this was my clearest sign of where the company was heading. There was this innovative technology called DSL—I know, I sound old. I knew at the time this was where I needed to be if I wanted to keep moving up the corporate ladder.

First, I figured out who the key players were on the DSL team and got uncomfortable. And by uncomfortable, I had to do something I normally wouldn't do. I had to get uncomfortable to get what I wanted. I had to figure out a way to get in front of someone I didn't know and tell them I wanted in on what they were doing.

I started to come up with a complex plan. Maybe I'll randomly run into him while eating lunch? Does he get coffee, and how often? I needed a plan. I worked this over and over in my head on what I wanted to do, and nothing seemed right. It all seemed fake, and if I could see through it, so could everyone else.

The more I thought about this and how I should do it, the more uncomfortable I was getting. Mainly because it felt fake, and I knew it.

Getting to the point of desperation, I did the most uncomfortable and spontaneous thing I could do, I sent a short and brief email. The email read as follows:

"Hi, Rob, I love what your team is doing, and I want to be part of it. Have time to connect so I can get on your radar? Let me know what works for you. Talk soon."

A FEW MINUTES LATER, I got a reply that read:

"Hey Frank, thanks for reaching out. I have copied my assistant, and she will find time for us to meet. Looking forward to it."

AFTER ALL THE stress of trying to figure out a plan, what I would do, and plotting, the best thing I did was the easiest.

Simple, straightforward, and concise. So, I had to get uncomfortable and do something I wouldn't normally do to get what I wanted—to get on his radar.

It took me finding out who the key players were and simply asking them to meet. It worked and continues to work for me. When you stop and think about this approach, the people you want to network with are busy and don't have time for the games. But ask them for something specific, ask them for action, and bam! Never would I have thought it would be that easy.

Later in life, I learned an important part of this kind of ask—the worst thing that can happen is they say, "No." Then you just move on to the next target or try again later.

If you are curious, I did get a job and moved teams. I spent the next few years in this group and continued to network internally.

The guy who hired me into the new team was an excellent coach and someone I admired and looked up to professionally. He once told me, "If you are planning to stay at the phone company, things are changing. You need to be in either internet or wireless."

I knew where I needed to be next, wireless.

At the same time, I had just started my MBA program, and quite a few people in this program worked for the same company as I did.

Again, I started by making a plan. And again, things didn't go as planned. I didn't learn from my earlier experience.

In this particular MBA program, we were grouped into teams. It is easy to get to know your team since you spend a good amount of time with them in breakout sessions and with certain assignments. The question then became, how do you get to know the other people in the program and what they do?

Well, that ended up being easier than I expected. There were these stupid icebreaker things some professors like to do, such as say your name, where you work, and what's your favorite animal. Bingo.

After a few rounds of this kind of icebreaker, which everyone hates, I found who I needed to connect with—they were my internal networking targets. Now, these folks weren't the end of the line because I wanted to get to their managers.

But I do not mean to discount any of these connections at all, because many of the people I connected with in the MBA program have lasted more than 20 years, and a few of them are good friends.

So back to the program. At the time, my goal was to get to a hiring manager. And by networking with my fellow students, over time, he became an advocate. And in the end, I didn't have to ask to meet with the hiring manager. I ended up being asked if I wanted to meet with him.

Again, I had to make myself uncomfortable. I didn't have a direct route to what I wanted and had to do things differently than I wanted. The result was what I wanted, but it wasn't the path I had planned out in my head. It never really is, and you need to have the flexibility to roll with it. Don't panic because things aren't going the way you thought.

Get uncomfortable and network internally.

But how does this help you outside of your current company? Great question. Again, people leave and go somewhere else. Sometimes, you may want to go with them, or sometimes they hear of other roles that might be a fit for you.

One of the people I met in my MBA program, someone

who has been a friend for nearly 20 years, has been a resource for new jobs and opportunities often. And to prove that the right connections last and prove fruitful, I ended up after all these years working for his ad agency.

The right connections internally can be a resource for short-term, i.e., internal opportunities and longer-term opportunities outside your current organization.

You just need to nurture these connections and don't let them go idle. Don't let them go too long without touching base. You need to connect with these folks even when you don't need anything. All it takes is a simple "Hey, just checking in to see how you are doing." Or, if you want to take your networking skills to the next level, ask them how you can help them. Be a team player. Be the person people want to help and return the favor—even before you are asked.

Some people hate asking for help, and if you offer it up first, without knowing if they need it, it builds a strong connection and likability.

You don't want to be known as the guy who only reaches out when he needs something. Again, have I done this? Yes. Why? Because I didn't know any better. Don't be like me. It is truly clear to the person on the other end, and it erodes your credibility.

Networking is like the first day of prison. What's the ongoing joke you hear all the time in the movies about your first day in prison? On your first day, find the biggest and meanest guy and knock him out. Well, networking internally is kind of like this. Granted, you don't knock anyone out nor pick any fights—at least not on the first day. But you should not avoid networking with people you are told are the "mean ones" or the office bully. If the gossip group doesn't tell you who it is, you'll find out soon enough.

What you should do is try to connect with these kinds of people and build an ally. This doesn't mean you have to agree with their behavior, and you need to keep an arm's length distance. You don't want to be one of "them," but you want to stay out of their wrath. Better to have them ignore you versus setting their sights on you or your work.

Now, you are probably asking, "Why would I do that?" You have probably, up until this point in your career, avoided people like this and felt it was the best strategy. Well, you are wrong.

There is a lot to learn from the office fool, plus you get information that you can use to your advantage. Are there downsides to this kind of networking—hell, yes. But let's cover the pros before the cons and maybe throw in a first-person story to help bring it together.

So, what are the pros? I have mentioned a few already. Information and not being on the receiving end all the time —because you will still get caught in the bully's crossfire, but less so.

Let's start with information. It is always good to know why people think this person is difficult to work with, and sometimes it is very self-evident why.

But proactively reaching out, it shows that you are different from the others. You will always, regardless of where you work, run into someone you can't stand or don't like to work with. You need to use this to your advantage.

First, don't talk about work, not unless you want to completely fail at connecting with this person. Find out something about them. This might be hard since most people like this tend to keep a lot of personal things close to their chest.

Second, try to connect outside of work. Ask them to lunch. Coffee. Just something away from the office. They may hate their job, and being in the office is not the right environment to connect.

The third is frequency. This effort is full-throated. You can't be one and done and expect a good result. You will most likely fail the first few times at connecting but keep at it.

The whole point is to get uncomfortable again.

This is a long-term play too. The more effort you make, the easier it will become later. Just stick with it. As part of this long-term play, you need to deploy expert-level emotional intelligence. Keep an eye on body language and words used. This applies to direct interactions and interactions in meetings or when others are present.

As you learn about where each person stands on projects or issues, navigate the waters carefully and cleverly. What you learn from your networking, use sparingly but wisely. This will help you as you grow professionally.

The enemy of my enemy is my friend. This suggests that two opposing parties should work together against a common enemy. The enemy in this scenario is the work to be done. Working with the "bad" guy to get stuff done isn't a terrible thing; you just need to be careful about how you do it to avoid hurting yourself.

But how can networking work for you? There have been times when I completely failed at this and a few times when it worked. A notable example of this was when I worked for a semi-startup e-commerce company. I say semi because it was more than ten years old at the time I joined and still called itself a startup. Granted, in many ways, it didn't act as a company that has been running for a decade.

Part of the reason I joined is that they were transitioning into hiring seasoned people to help them grow. As part of this, they hired a lot of folks with considerable experience across almost every department. I was responsible at the time for all of consumer direct marketing, which included all the e-commerce marketing.

About two years into my role, they decided to hire a VP in another department. He would be a peer, so to speak, or at least someone I would have to work with almost daily. He owned the products; I owned the marketing. We would be pretty much hand in hand. His success and my success were tied.

Do you know what the biggest problem is with hiring experienced people from outside of a small organization? Yep, culture—and the constant thought that everyone here is an idiot. He was mostly right on the latter.

He was smart. He knew what he was doing. He knew what he wanted to do, and those who didn't get on board were steamrolled. Abrasive? Yes. Confident? Yes. I liked him.

There wasn't a meeting that didn't go by where people would come to me afterward and complain or ask me in a frantic voice, "What are you going to do?"

It was obvious that I needed to connect with him mainly because my job sort of depended on us getting stuff done.

I connected. I worked it from every angle. I built a personal relationship, so the working relationship would go smoother. Did I ruffle his feathers? Yes, when I needed to. But getting to know him on a personal level and making the effort to network with him almost continuously, I was able to learn the go/no go areas. I learned when to push back and when to hold.

My team didn't understand. They just thought he was a jerk. They would ask me, "Why didn't you say something to him in the meeting?" My answer would be, "Because it wasn't the right time, and I will address my concerns privately."

I knew, at a given meeting, if I said something, it would have been a clown show. Because I took the time to understand his personality and to deploy my expert emotional intelligence, I knew to lose the fight and regroup privately to win the war.

Most people, when attacked, either shrink or fight back. When dealing with a personality like this, they feed off both of those. But if you retreated and attacked later in a safer environment, you'd be surprised by the results.

See, I learned through my efforts that ego and feelings were important to this VP. He wanted to be perceived as if he were in charge and he was the one making the decisions. Challenge that and expect wrath.

But take your concerns privately and have a new plan; you'll make headway and get things done.

Having this flexibility is one thing, but the need to internally network with abrasive people has its benefits.

We would often have lunch. Conversions in our offices. We built a relationship that most would have avoided because of the behavior. Don't avoid it. Embrace it and make it work for you. This kind of internal networking is important, and most don't do it because it makes them uncomfortable.

There are pitfalls of networking, and I am not talking about the video game. Granted, some of you might not even understand the reference—not that I care. Now, let's move to the flipside of this "success" story and talk about the cons, of which there are many.

One big drawback to trying to network with difficult people internally is that it might just not work. Meaning the person just may not be open to wanting to connect with you. They could be completely checked out and don't give a lick about wanting to connect. They just check the box at work every day. This person is Po-Po, as compared to a Hi-Po. Po-Po is Passed over and Pissed Off. No matter how hard you try, no matter how long you try, you'll never make any headway.

This is ok. It is not your fault, but be smart and have the emotional intelligence to know when to move on.

Another pitfall is being seen by others as being like the office jerk. Always being seen with that person and seeming to agree at times. All the unruly behavior that people can associate you with and project onto you.

Again, emotional intelligence is key to avoiding this, but it won't stop some people from associating you with the other person. Be mindful of this. Make efforts to go to lunch with other people as well. If you stop by someone's office, do it to others as well. Distribute your internal networking evenly or nearly evenly.

You can't change the way people think, but you can influence it with your behavior. You need to be able to juggle multiple relationships internally while reaching your goals. I believe the benefits outweigh the cons of this kind of networking.

Internal networking is both a long- and short-term play, meaning it can help even after you leave an organization. In the short term, it can help you get work done, such as connecting with the office antagonizer.

Your internal networking should focus on people outside of your department or direct line of sight. Reach out across the organization when possible. I know in smaller organizations, that simply means looking across the room to see everyone.

But in those situations, find the key influencers and step

up to take on tasks outside of your day-to-day and even your comfort zone. Make the best of it and use it to your advantage.

In a larger organization, you have plenty of opportunities to find and connect with people in and out of your local office. You just need to have a plan.

Plan the work, work the plan. That is what I was told almost every day when I worked for one of the Big Four account/consulting firms. Every day. The same applies here. Plan your internal networking strategy. Then work the plan.

Make yourself uncomfortable and find a way to connect with the right people both internally and externally.

Stop posting inspirational quotes and start to inspire people with your own quotes and thoughts. If you want to connect with the right people, then start acting in a way that draws them in versus pushing them away.

And for the love of God, stop ruining LinkedIn.

12

OFFICE POLITICS IS A FULL CONTACT SPORT

I n the world of business, there is an old saying: *You either play office politics or you don't. There is no in-between.* If you want to move up the ladder and increase your chances for promotion, then it is something that cannot be ignored. Some people would argue that playing this game can be damaging and backfire on you, but others say if done correctly, it can be beneficial and help them to their positions.

A simple definition is that office politics refers to the complex dynamics and power struggles that occur within a workplace. It involves the use of influence, power, and networking to achieve goals, gain advantages, and advance one's interests.

Although many people see office politics as nothing more than office gossip, backstabbing co-workers, and general office bullying—this is not necessarily true, but it does happen more often than most would like. It tends to be perceived as negative, and although it is often the case, there is room for you to navigate it to your benefit. So how can you do this?

Most office politics is based around office relationships. People work better with people they like and get on well with, so if you aim to be an office politician, then you need to win people over. This does not mean that you must become best buddies with everyone at the office, but it does help. A little office politicking goes a long way in this game. You don't necessarily need to form friendships, but just make sure people are nice when they talk about you or discuss situations involving you.

Here are some top tips for office politics:

- **Make yourself invaluable**. If there is one thing worse than someone playing office politics, it's someone who takes all the credit while making it look effortless and like everyone is wasting their time. There is never a point in office politics where you want to fail. If there is an important task that needs completing or anything you can do to help with office politics then take on the challenge. If people value your contribution and keep noticing how often you go above and beyond for co-workers, then office politicking can't be all bad.

- **Keep things positive**. This isn't always possible, but it does work most of the time. No one likes office politicians who constantly moan about how busy they are, complain about workloads, and generally moan about everything going on around them. It gets very tiresome and makes people wonder why on earth they bother playing office politics. Everyone has a bad day from time to time, but office politics is not the place for them.

- **Don't spread office gossip**. This may seem like a no-brainer, but office politics can be easy to get involved in and take part in, even if you don't mean for it to happen. It doesn't have to be malicious gossip, either. Office politics is often built on casual chats between colleagues. The last thing you want to do is take part in any office politics that could reflect badly on yourself or anyone else you work with because it will just backfire in a big way. If something is going on around the office, then stay out of it unless someone really needs your help.

- **Leave office politics at the office**. Getting involved in office politics can be a double-edged sword. You need to know when to take yourself out of it without being too obvious about it. It is difficult to completely remove yourself from office politics, but if you stick with removing yourself from office gossip and office drama, then this will help you to do so quite quickly. If your aim is office politicking, then it does not look good on you if all you seem interested in doing is complaining about or criticizing other people who are playing office politics. Sooner or later, people will realize office politics can be one of those things that, if treated properly, can work for their benefit. Just make sure everyone is getting something out of it, and it should not be too difficult.

AGAIN, at its core, office politics is a form of office behavior that involves influencing or working with others without them realizing that this is what you are doing. And while it has been said that office politics is no more than office gossip, backstabbing co-workers, and general office bullying—this is not necessarily true, but it does happen more often than most would like.

Office politics may be a dirty game, but once everyone knows what is going on there tends to be a sort of equilibrium where one person does not take over. If office politics brings out the worst in people, then you need to take a step back and try to concentrate on office politics that are office friendly.

Office politics can bring out the worst in people because office politics simplifies office behavior. To succeed in office politics, you do not need everyone's support, but you do need their tolerance. This is also true of office friendships. However, office politicking is no place for friendship unless your friendship is office friendly.

Every office has its fair share of office politicians who will try to manipulate situations to suit themselves or to make themselves look good. They take credit for others' achievements without even saying, "Thank you," or doing anything that might indicate that they are being kind or helpful to others.

If you are playing office politics, then chances are several others are playing it, so you have a certain level of competition to take into consideration when office politicking.

If office politics makes you look bad or is making your work life less productive or less fun, then maybe office politics isn't the right avenue for you. This is especially true if office politics make a lot of people generally unhappy because office politics can draw in several non-office political players and office poison.

The best players in office politics are usually those who have been around the office for a long time and know how things work in an office environment. But even these people will only create positive change for themselves (or their friends), never negative change based on office politics, because once everyone knows what they are doing, it can backfire very quickly. That will make other people think twice about office politics.

Office politics is like office gossip in that office gossip is not always office politicking. It can be something someone overheard or saw in passing, but office gossip does tend to lean toward politicking at the office.

The best way to avoid office politics is to keep your head down and do what you do best without taking credit for anything because if another person tries to take credit for an idea or project of yours, this could lead to office drama very quickly. If there are office political players in the game, then choosing not to play them will usually make them look worse than you. It might distract people from other possible office politicians who may be playing a different version of the same game—most likely using office poison as their weapon of choice.

Office politics can be a very useful tool to have in your office communication arsenal, but office politics can also have a lot of office fallout. Thus, it is best not to take office politics too seriously and to keep track of office gossip as well as any office drama that might start as a result. It never hurts to document office happenings just in case you need to use them as leverage against office political players who just don't seem to want to play nice. Just remember, the best way to handle office politics is from the background—this means office politicking without office politicians knowing you are doing it. Only then will you be able to fully utilize all the benefits that come with playing this game.

Office politics can have a major impact on employee morale and can lead to a toxic work environment. The constant competition and maneuvering for power and control can create an atmosphere of distrust and suspicion, leading to increased stress and decreased job satisfaction for employees. This can cause a loss of motivation and commitment to the job, leading to a decrease in productivity and an increase in absenteeism.

In a politically charged workplace, employees are often more concerned with pleasing their superiors and protecting their self-interests rather than working together for the betterment of the company. This can lead to a lack of cooperation and collaboration, making it difficult to achieve common goals and leading to missed deadlines and reduced quality of work.

Moreover, office politics can lead to discrimination, favoritism, and unequal treatment of employees. Those who are perceived as having more power and influence are often given preferential treatment, while others are excluded and ostracized. This can lead to feelings of injustice and can cause employees to lose trust in their superiors and the company as a whole.

Overall, office politics can have a major impact on employee morale and can lead to a toxic work environment. Companies need to take steps to address and prevent office politics to maintain a positive and productive workplace. This can include creating a code of conduct that promotes transparency and fairness, encouraging open communication and collaboration, and promoting a culture of respect and trust. By doing so, companies can foster a positive work environment that supports employee well-being and promotes success.

The negative impact of office politics on employee morale can lead to higher employee turnover and reduced employee retention. In a toxic work environment, employees are more likely to become disengaged and dissatisfied with their job, leading to a higher likelihood of quitting or seeking employment elsewhere. This results in higher turnover, which can be costly for the company in terms of both time and resources spent on recruiting and training new employees.

Moreover, office politics can also have a major impact on employee retention. Employees who feel that they are being unfairly treated or discriminated against are more likely to leave their job, regardless of their overall satisfaction with the company. In a politically charged work environment, employees are less likely to feel valued and supported, which can lead to a lack of motivation and a decreased sense of commitment to the company.

Additionally, office politics can also lead to a lack of trust and confidence in leadership, making it difficult to retain employees who may feel that their superiors are not acting in their best interests. This can lead to increased stress and decreased job satisfaction, which can be particularly damaging to employee retention, as employees are more likely to seek employment elsewhere in search of a more supportive and positive work environment.

Therefore, companies need to address and prevent office politics to maintain a positive work environment and reduce the risk of higher employee turnover and reduced employee retention. By creating a culture of respect, fairness, and transparency, companies can foster a positive work environment that supports employee well-being and promotes success.

Surprisingly, there could be some benefits of office politics, although it is mostly negative. I guess, in some ways, the pros could be the following:

- **Facilitates decision-making**: It enables individuals to make decisions that are in their best interest and the organization's goals.
- **Provides visibility and opportunities**: It provides a platform for individuals to showcase their talents, skills, and abilities and gain recognition from higher-ups.
- **Enhances communication**: Office politics can help create open channels of communication between employees and management.
- **Can foster healthy competition**: Competition can spur employees to work harder, innovate, and perform better.
- **Can lead to positive changes**: Individuals can use office politics to push for changes that benefit the organization.

BUT AGAIN, I think the cons outweigh the pros:

- **Can lead to toxic work environments**: Office politics can lead to backstabbing, gossiping, and favoritism, leading to a toxic work environment that can affect productivity and morale.

- **Can create divisions and conflicts**: It can create divisions and conflicts within teams, affecting team cohesion and the achievement of goals.
- **Can hinder decision-making**: It can hinder decision-making as individuals may prioritize their interests over the organization's goals, leading to suboptimal outcomes.
- **Can lead to unethical behavior**: Office politics can lead to unethical behavior such as lying, cheating, and manipulation, leading to a loss of trust and credibility.
- **Can stifle creativity**: It can stifle creativity and innovation as employees may be more focused on impressing their superiors than on developing new ideas.

OVERALL, while office politics can have some benefits, it's important to be aware of its potential negative impacts and try to navigate it in a way that fosters a healthy and productive work environment.

The concept of office politics involves the use of influence, power, and networking to achieve goals, gain advantages, and advance one's interests in the workplace. While some argue that playing office politics can be beneficial to one's career growth, others see it as damaging and potentially backfiring.

Office politics can create a negative and toxic work environment, leading to decreased employee morale, reduced job satisfaction, and higher employee turnover.

Although there may be some benefits of office politics, such as facilitating decision-making and providing opportunities for recognition and healthy competition, its potential negative impacts, such as divisions and conflicts, unethical behavior, and a stifling of creativity, outweigh the pros.

Companies should take steps to address and prevent office politics, such as promoting transparency, fairness, and a culture of respect and trust, to foster a positive and productive work environment that supports employee well-being and promotes success.

13

TRUST

Trust is a fundamental aspect of any successful business, and it begins with building strong relationships with those around you. As a professional, it's important to establish trust with coworkers, superiors, and clients to effectively achieve business goals. This chapter will explore the importance of trust in the workplace, how to build trust through relationship building, and strategies for overcoming mistrust and rebuilding trust in a toxic environment.

Trust is a powerful asset that can positively impact all aspects of a business. If you want to get things done as effectively as possible, you need to build trust with those around you who will help you accomplish those tasks. This means building relationships with people who trust you. You trust them, verifying trust through a trust circle, remaining equitable in your dealings with others, and being fair with the information you're given as well as with the requests you make of others.

Relationship building is the first step in building trust in the workplace. This involves getting to know your coworkers and superiors on a personal level and establishing open and honest communication. One effective way to build relationships is to become familiar with executive assistants. These individuals typically have a good understanding of what's happening throughout the company and can be an excellent source of information about a particular department or process. To maintain trust within this group, it's important to be fair and treat others equally. Avoid shutting down someone because they don't have any information for you, as this can create a rift in the trust circle. Remember, the more trust you give out, the more trust people will give back to you.

It's important to note that trust can be eroded, and sometimes, it may be difficult to trust those you work with. When trust is eroded, it can lead to poor communication, low morale, and decreased productivity. If you find yourself in this situation, there are steps you can take to try to restore trust. First, it's important to identify the reasons why you are having difficulties trusting others. This could be due to past experiences, misunderstandings, or other factors. Understanding the root causes of your trust issues can help you address them more effectively.

Next, consider having an open and honest conversation with the individuals you have difficulties trusting. Express your concerns and try to understand their perspective. This can help to clear up misunderstandings and build a deeper understanding and respect for each other. If the situation is more serious, it may be necessary to involve a neutral third party, such as a manager or HR representative, to mediate the conversation and help resolve the issue.

In some cases, it may be necessary to re-establish boundaries and set clear expectations for communication and collaboration. This can include setting specific goals, developing clear protocols for decision-making and problem-solving, and establishing clear lines of responsibility. Finally, it's important to be patient and persistent in your efforts to rebuild trust. Trust takes time to develop and can be easily eroded, so it's important to make a continuous effort to maintain it.

When trust is eroded or if you have difficulties trusting those you work with, it's important to identify the reasons, have open and honest conversations, involve a neutral third party, if necessary, re-establish boundaries and expectations, and be patient and persistent in your efforts to rebuild trust. By taking these steps, you can help to restore trust and create a positive work environment.

Building trust in the workplace is essential for creating a positive and productive work environment. Trust is the foundation for successful teamwork and communication, as well as for building strong relationships between coworkers and management. One of the most important ways to build trust in the workplace is to be honest and transparent. This means being truthful about your intentions, actions, and decisions, and being open about your thoughts and feelings. It also means being honest about any mistakes you make and taking responsibility for your actions. This level of openness and honesty builds credibility and shows that you are a trustworthy person.

Another way to build trust in the workplace is to keep your promises and commitments. When you make a promise, it's important to follow through on it, as this builds trust and reliability. This applies to small commitments, such as meeting deadlines, as well as larger commitments, such as taking on a new project.

In addition to being honest and keeping your promises, it's also important to be respectful and empathetic towards your coworkers. This means actively listening to their concerns and opinions, valuing their contributions, and treating them with dignity and respect. When coworkers feel heard and valued, they are more likely to trust and respect you in return.

Furthermore, building trust in the workplace also involves being supportive and helpful to your coworkers. Whether it's offering to help with a task or being a sounding board for a coworker's ideas, taking the time to support and help your coworkers builds trust and strengthens relationships.

Building trust in the workplace requires honesty, reliability, respect, and support. When everyone in the workplace works together to build and maintain trust, it creates a positive and productive work environment that benefits everyone.

To establish trust within the workplace, it is important to recognize the different factors that contribute to the creation of a toxic work environment. One of the biggest contributors is a lack of communication. In a workplace where people do not communicate effectively, misunderstandings can occur, and this can lead to mistrust between employees.

Another factor that contributes to a toxic work environment is a lack of recognition or appreciation for the efforts of others. When people feel that their efforts are not appreciated, it can lead to resentment and mistrust, as people may feel that they are being taken advantage of.

Micromanagement is another factor that can lead to a toxic work environment. When employees feel that they are being micromanaged, it can lead to a lack of trust between employees and their managers.

To overcome these obstacles and build trust within the

workplace it's important to establish clear lines of communication. This means encouraging open and honest dialogue between employees and managers, as well as between coworkers. Managers should provide regular feedback to their employees and offer recognition for their efforts. This can be achieved through regular performance evaluations, as well as using incentives or rewards for exceptional performance.

In addition to providing regular feedback, managers need to delegate tasks effectively. This means providing employees with clear instructions, as well as giving them the autonomy to complete tasks in their own way. When employees feel that they have control over their work and are trusted to make their own decisions, it can lead to a more positive work environment and increased productivity.

Another way to build trust within the workplace is to create a culture of transparency. This means being open and honest about company policies and decisions, as well as about the company's financial status. When employees feel that they have a clear understanding of the company's goals and objectives, it can lead to a greater sense of trust and loyalty.

Finally, managers need to lead by example. This means demonstrating the values and behaviors that they want to see in their employees. When managers are honest, reliable, respectful, and supportive, it sets the tone for the rest of the organization and helps to build a culture of trust and cooperation.

Trust is a fundamental aspect of any successful business, and it begins with building strong relationships with those around you. Building trust in the workplace requires honesty, reliability, respect, and support. It also involves recognizing the different factors that contribute to a toxic work environment and taking steps to overcome them. By establishing clear lines of communication, providing regular feedback, delegating tasks effectively, creating a culture of transparency, and leading by example, you can help to build a positive and productive work environment that is built on a foundation of trust.

It's also important to remember that trust is not something that can be built overnight. It takes time and effort to establish trust with others, and it can be easily eroded if not properly maintained. It's important to make a continuous effort to maintain trust by consistently demonstrating honesty, reliability, respect, and support.

In addition, it's important to recognize that trust is a two-way street. Just as you want others to trust you, you must also be willing to trust others. This means being open and receptive to new ideas and being willing to take calculated risks when necessary. When you trust others, you empower them to make decisions and take ownership of their work, which can lead to increased productivity and a more positive work environment.

Ultimately, trust is an essential ingredient for any successful business. When trust is established and maintained within the workplace, it can lead to greater collaboration, improved communication, and increased productivity. By building trust with those around you, you can help to create a positive and productive work environment that benefits everyone. So, take the time to invest in building trust, and watch as your business flourishes.

Trust is a vital component of any successful workplace. It is the foundation upon which effective collaboration, communication, and productivity are built. Trust is an asset that benefits everyone in the workplace, from employees and managers to clients and customers. In this section, we will explore how trust benefits everyone (pros) in the workplace and also the downsides (cons) of trust.

PROS OF TRUST in the Workplace

- **Improved Communication**: Trust facilitates open and honest communication. When people trust one another, they are more likely to share their thoughts, feelings, and ideas without fear of judgment or negative repercussions. This leads to better communication and collaboration, which in turn leads to improved decision-making and problem-solving.
- **Increased Productivity**: Trust also leads to increased productivity. When people trust one another, they are more likely to work together effectively and efficiently. They are also more likely to take initiative and be proactive, which leads to greater productivity and achievement of goals.
- **Enhanced Innovation**: Trust encourages creativity and innovation. When people trust one another, they are more willing to take risks and try new things. They are also more likely to share their ideas and collaborate on new projects, leading to the development of innovative solutions and approaches.
- **Better Relationships**: Trust leads to better relationships. When people trust one another, they are more likely to build strong, positive relationships based on mutual respect and

understanding. This creates a more positive and supportive work environment, which in turn leads to greater job satisfaction and higher morale.

- **Greater Loyalty**: Trust also leads to greater loyalty. When people trust their colleagues and managers, they are more likely to stay with the company and be committed to its success. This leads to reduced turnover, which saves the company time and money in recruiting and training new employees.

Cons of Trust in the Workplace

- **Vulnerability to Deception**: One of the major cons of trust is the vulnerability to deception. When people trust others, they may be more likely to believe what they are told without questioning it. This can lead to being deceived or misled by others.
- **Time-consuming**: Building trust takes time and effort. It requires consistent actions and behaviors over an extended period. This can be time-consuming and may require a significant investment of time and resources.
- **Risk of Betrayal**: Trust can be broken if someone acts in a way that violates the trust that has been established. This can be devastating and can have long-lasting negative effects on relationships and productivity.
- **Reduced Objectivity**: When people trust one another, they may be more likely to overlook

flaws or weaknesses in their colleagues or managers. This can lead to reduced objectivity and a lack of constructive criticism or feedback, which can ultimately hinder individual and organizational growth.

- **Difficulty in Regaining Trust**: Once trust has been broken, it can be difficult to regain it. It requires a significant amount of effort and time to rebuild trust, and some relationships may never fully recover.

DESPITE THESE POTENTIAL DRAWBACKS, the benefits of trust in the workplace far outweigh the cons. Trust is an essential ingredient for a positive and productive work environment, and it is worth the effort to invest in building and maintaining it.

TIPS FOR BUILDING Trust in the Workplace

- **Be Honest and Transparent**: Honesty and transparency are the building blocks of trust. Be truthful about your intentions, actions, and decisions, and be open about your thoughts and feelings. Also, be honest about any mistakes you make and take responsibility for your actions.
- **Keep Your Promises**: When you make a promise, follow through on it. This builds trust and reliability and shows that you are a dependable and trustworthy person.
- **Listen Actively**: Active listening is essential for building trust. Pay attention to what others are

saying, show empathy and understanding, and take their opinions and feelings into consideration.

- **Show Respect**: Treating others with respect and dignity is key to building trust. Listen to their concerns, value their contributions, and avoid actions or words that may be perceived as dismissive or disrespectful.
- **Be Supportive**: Offer support and help to your colleagues when needed. This shows that you are a team player and helps to build trust and strengthen relationships.
- **Forgive Past Mistakes**: Forgiving past mistakes is important for building trust. Holding grudges and dwelling on past issues can create an environment of mistrust, so it's important to let go of past mistakes and focus on moving forward.
- **Practice Patience**: Trust takes time to build, so it's important to be patient and persistent in your efforts to build trust. Keep in mind that trust can easily be eroded and hard to repair.

TRUST IS a powerful asset in the workplace that benefits everyone involved. Building and maintaining trust takes effort and time, but the benefits are well worth it. By following these tips and practicing honesty, reliability, respect, and support, you can help to create a positive and productive work environment built on a foundation of trust.

14

THE 3 E'S

W hat I find interesting about running marketing campaigns, whether it be for online acquisition, branding, retail promotions, or product launch, is that most people do not follow or have standard processes for complete campaign management. Granted, they may have processes for one aspect or another, but are they all connected?

Even more interesting, most people do not apply this same methodology to their professional careers. So, hear me out; let's start with the concept of campaign management, but you really could insert any kind of project. It doesn't need to be a marketing campaign.

The key is to find best practices and repeat those successful actions. Oddly, the same could be said about your professional growth. This will lead to end-to-end solid campaign management processes. When I was working in telco, focused on national promotions, I had a mantra of the three E's—Evolution, Execution, and Evaluation. Each step feeds the next and cycles endlessly, feeding the next campaign and allowing you to take the best practices into the next campaign. This allows you to continually develop the next big idea.

Evolution feeds execution. Knowing what you need to accomplish or want to accomplish is key. Having specific goals, more importantly, having specific, measurable goals, feeds the Evaluation phase. Knowing how you performed or where there are areas for improvement allows you to evolve the next idea into something more successful.

These steps do not need to wait for the end of the campaign either. Doing continuous evaluation while you are executing will allow you to optimize the campaign and feed the evolution of new ideas or changes. Taking those optimizations and executing on them will help campaigns find the sweet spot for success.

Now this seems simple and something everyone should know about. But how many companies or agencies actually do this? Everyone talks about postmortem meetings, and they talk about how ideas are developed, but does anyone ever talk about how each step is connected? Does anyone look at the postmortem information and make actionable changes? From my experience, the answer is "No." The three E's create an environment where the "No" becomes a "Yes!"

Regardless of your processes, they fit into one of the three E's. The challenge is finding out how they are connected. If you can figure that out and can repeat them consistently, you will be able to identify successful campaigns from the ones that should be changed or dumped.

Connecting it to your personal growth and career, the steps to executing and evaluating projects and campaigns are similar in style. Take a project or campaign and break it down into Initiation, Planning, Execution, Operation (people/team), Evaluation, and Implementation (purpose).

The Initiation phase consists of identifying either project opportunities or potential project ideas. This can be done by using framework tools such as SWOT analysis or Canvas Analysis to help get the project team organized on what they need to accomplish. This helps them understand how their work will have an impact on project outcomes.

In the Planning phase, project teams can build project plans based on project initiation. Standard project management tools such as PRINCE2 project methodologies or iterative and incremental project planning techniques such as SCRUM help you to ensure systematic project plan creation and execution.

Execution helps the project teams figure out what they need to do and how they need to achieve their goals. This includes communication, coordination of people/teams, and execution of work packages. The key here is repetition in this process, allowing for continuous improvement and evolution of the campaign plan into something more effective. For that, specific project team members ensure communication cascades throughout the organization to increase the likelihood of project success. Also, during this step, you identify the potential people who will be located from both inside your organization and outside of it for communication. The key to this step is less about what everyone does and more about how everyone communicates with each other.

Evaluation, like project evaluation, should be continuous throughout the project (campaign). The key difference is that project management evaluations are usually done at the project end, while marketing campaign evaluations need to happen continuously throughout the project/campaign life cycle. This provides opportunities for actionable insights which feed back into either your project plan or your campaign execution plan. These insights provide you with information about opportunity changes and potential risks before they derail your project or campaign completely. This will help you evolve your project opportunities and change any plans accordingly to keep on track with project objectives. Since this process frequently occurs during both the Planning and Execution phases, it should be clearly communicated through all levels of communication cascades within an organization (company), allowing for project (campaign) execution to be more effective by better-aligning project/campaign objectives, project constraints, project deliverables, project risks, and project benefits.

Human Resources are important in both project management and marketing. One of the big differences is that with project management, you use project resources (employees) for a specific task(s) or projects, whereas in marketing, your human resource assets help drive an entire campaign. This considers the short-term assignments with each team member's skillset along with a long-term alloca-tion of talent, which provides a good balance between continuity and change as well as project goals. The key here is allocating your talent based on the potential impact it can have on a given project opportunity or campaign. Assign them to a different project (campaign) that can be imple-mented within your organization (company). Stakeholders are also important for project (campaign) success. Stake-holders act as project beneficiaries, providing project teams with insights about the project opportunity, project constraints, project risks, and project benefits so team members better understand how their project work takes impacts these things.

This 5-phase campaign execution model helps you think through all the elements needed to execute a successful marketing campaign—from planning and preparation to launch and evaluation. The five phases are Initiation, Planning, Execution, Refinement & Optimization, and Evaluation. Though it's represented by steps 1–5 here, none of these phases happen in isolation or in any order. You'll go back and forth between some of the phases as you learn more about your project team's project (marketing campaign) needs.

Broadly speaking, project management is about helping people to produce effective projects that deliver value to an organization by ensuring project objectives are met or exceeded. In marketing terms, this means you want a project that meets or exceeds customer expectations in a timeline that fits into the company's overall product/brand strategy, all while staying within budget constraints. The project manager has two primary roles: One role is focused on managing relationships with their project stakeholders and project team members, including promoting clear communication among them throughout a project. The second role is focused on making sure a project runs successfully from start to finish. Stakeholders are project beneficiaries, the people who have a vested interest in project success. Stakeholders can be internal or external to an organization—or both. Marketing project manager roles are like project management work with roles including project manager, project coordinator, project scheduler, project assistant, and marketing analyst. There are no formal titles for project management positions within an organization (company), although some companies may use some of these job titles interchangeably.

The following is some more information on common project manager responsibilities:

- They help plan and coordinate projects, whether they are marketing campaigns or development projects. Treat them the same way.
- They keep track of budget details.
- They sometimes act as liaisons between teams.
- They're responsible for delivering relevant reports on campaign progress.

THE KEY IS to focus on the 3 E's—Evolution of the ideas, Execution of the ideas, and Evaluating how well everything went.

Thinking deeper about execution and the basics of the principle, what does it really mean? Well, Execution is the process of turning a project plan into reality and achieving the desired outcomes. It is a critical aspect of project management and a key factor in the success or failure of a project.

Effective execution requires clear communication, efficient resource allocation, and strict adherence to project schedules and budgets. Project managers must balance competing demands and make informed decisions that keep the project moving forward. They must also be able to anticipate and resolve obstacles as they arise, ensuring that the project stays on track.

The success of a project depends on the quality of its execution. Poor execution can result in delays, cost overruns, and substandard results. On the other hand, well-executed projects deliver results that meet or exceed expectations and are completed within budget and on time.

In addition, good execution practices foster a culture of accountability and responsibility, helping to build trust and credibility with stakeholders. It also helps to ensure that projects align with the organization's goals and objectives and contribute to its long-term success.

Effective execution is essential for successful project outcomes. Project managers play a crucial role in ensuring that projects are executed efficiently and effectively, delivering results that meet or exceed stakeholder expectations.

Being adaptable is a valuable quality in project management as it allows for quick and effective responses to changing circumstances and unexpected events. In a project environment, unexpected challenges and obstacles are common, and the ability to adapt to these changes can mean the difference between success and failure.

An adaptable project manager can pivot their approach as needed, considering new information, shifting priorities, or changes in resources. They are also able to identify and make use of new opportunities that emerge, helping to keep the project moving forward.

Adaptability also helps to foster a culture of flexibility and collaboration within the project team. Teams that can respond quickly to changing circumstances and adjust their approach are more likely to be successful in delivering projects on time and within budget.

Additionally, being adaptable can also help to maintain stakeholder buy-in and support, even in the face of changes or challenges. Project managers who can demonstrate their ability to respond to unexpected events and keep the project moving forward are more likely to earn the trust and confidence of stakeholders.

The ability to be adaptable is a crucial aspect of successful project management. By being flexible and responsive to changing circumstances, project managers can ensure that projects are delivered on time, within budget, and to the satisfaction of stakeholders.

When a project is going off track, it is important to quickly assess the situation and determine the root cause of the problem. This information can be gathered through regular progress updates, project reviews, and communication with team members and stakeholders.

Once the cause of the problem is identified, the project manager can take the following steps to get the project back on track:

1. **Develop a recovery plan**: This should include steps to address the root cause of the problem, reallocate resources as needed, and get the project back on schedule.
2. **Communicate with stakeholders**: Keep stakeholders informed of the situation, the steps being taken to address it, and the expected outcome. This helps to maintain transparency and build trust.
3. **Prioritize tasks**: Review the project plan and prioritize tasks based on their impact on the overall project schedule and budget.
4. **Reassess resource allocation**: Ensure that the right resources are available and utilized effectively to get the project back on track.
5. **Monitor progress and adjust the recovery plan as needed**: Regularly track progress and adjust

the recovery plan as needed to ensure that the project stays on track.

IT IS important to remember that a project going off track is not necessarily a failure. With the right approach and a focus on finding solutions, it is possible to get the project back on track and achieve a successful outcome.

When a project is going off track, the project manager must take quick action to assess the situation, develop a recovery plan, communicate with stakeholders, prioritize tasks, reassess resource allocation, and monitor progress. With these steps, it is possible to get the project back on track and achieve a successful outcome.

Getting people onboard with your vision for a project, its charter, goals, and outcomes is critical to the success of the project. Here are some steps that you can take to achieve this:

1. **Communicate clearly**: Clearly articulate the project vision, charter, goals, and outcomes to all stakeholders, including team members and upper management. This helps to ensure that everyone is on the same page and has a clear understanding of what is expected.

2. **Involve stakeholders in the planning process**: Encourage stakeholder participation in the planning process. This helps to build buy-in and commitment to the project, as stakeholders are more likely to support something that they have had a hand in creating.

3. **Align the project with organizational goals**: Ensure that the project is aligned with the organization's goals and objectives. This helps to build support from upper management and demonstrates the value that the project will bring to the organization.

4. **Demonstrate the benefits of the project**: Communicate the benefits of the project to stakeholders. This could include cost savings, increased productivity, improved customer satisfaction, or enhanced competitiveness.

5. **Lead by example**: As the project manager, it is important to demonstrate your commitment to the project and lead by example. Show enthusiasm and a positive attitude and encourage others to do the same.

6. **Provide regular updates**: Regularly update stakeholders on the progress of the project and be transparent about any challenges or obstacles that arise. This helps to build trust and confidence in the project and encourages stakeholders to continue to support it.

GETTING people onboard with your vision for a project, its charter, goals, and outcomes requires clear communication, stakeholder involvement, alignment with organizational goals, demonstration of benefits, strong leadership, and regular updates. By taking these steps, you can build buy-in and commitment from stakeholders and increase the chances of project success.

AFTERWORD

At the beginning of this book, I spoke about contradictions. Being successful at work requires a lot more than just being smart. It takes practice and effort. The same is true about being successful outside of work. It takes effort and practice to be successful in life, which brings me to my final tip on working smart:

Success requires the courage to fail. You can't do anything without failing first. If you are not afraid of failure, you are doing something wrong. The anxiety of failure causes people to become unable to take risks or try at all. If you want success, you must learn how to cope with failing because it will happen throughout your life—guaranteed!

Focus on Being Prepared, Not Just Smart

Everyone needs a road map and the right tools for the job — even geniuses — so why not prepare and use them? This book has demonstrated that although intelligence is important, it's not the only factor.

Being prepared means you have done everything in your power to ensure success before an event starts or before you need something. It doesn't mean that when things go wrong, you will be able to do the perfect thing and make everything work out in the end.

In life, if you think of yourself as a project manager, your main priority is your team and making sure everyone knows their role and how they can help with achieving goals. If someone on the team is falling behind or going off course, you need to keep them motivated until they are back on track or find a replacement for that individual. This might not be easy because trust breaks down when there isn't a good leader in place. People can't be expected to do their best when they don't trust the person in charge and feel like no one is looking out for them.

The introduction of emotional intelligence has been a major shift in how success has been viewed by some experts, but for others, it is still all about IQ and hard work. To these people, talent or ability is what separates successful from unsuccessful people; however, there's more to life than cold facts and numbers on a piece of paper.

Success at any level takes trust and teamwork, not just smarts. Have faith that you are equipped with everything you need to reach the top. Learn how to communicate well with your team members so you can keep moving forward toward your goals instead of beating yourself up over past mistakes. If something doesn't work out, then quickly switch directions and try a different path to achieve your objective. You aren't going to get it right the first time every time—no one does—but if you keep trying, eventually, you will find your way. Once you do, people will see the hard work you've put in and be able to follow in your footsteps because they can relate to what you have been through.

Being a leader is a lot like overseeing any other project. You can't just tell everyone what to do and expect them to automatically follow your every command. If the relationship isn't based on trust, people will be too worried about what you are going to say or think when they make mistakes. They won't feel comfortable coming up with their own ideas because they'll think it's not good enough.

The best approach is to encourage independent thinking while still monitoring progress and making sure people don't get off course. When someone tries, they should know that you appreciate the hard work even if the results aren't what they were aiming for in the end.

Leading by example is always better than trying to force people to do things. If you need help, then ask for it. Don't be afraid that people will think less of you because they don't see you as a know-it-all any longer. Having faith in your abilities and showing everyone around you that you can turn a bad situation into a good thing is enough to make them remember who the ultimate leader is.

Being confident about your ideas and not afraid to give them a try means more people will want to work with you instead of against you. When someone has an idea, encourage it, even if it's not the best one on paper. Always look at what can be done as opposed to what can't or shouldn't have been suggested in the first place.

For example, if someone wants to hold a party but it isn't the best time of the year, don't be afraid to tell them so. Ask questions like "What's your goal for this event?" or "Is there another way we can achieve what you want to do?"

Show your support by explaining why their great idea might not be as good as they think it is and then suggest other ways that might work better. It takes courage to admit that something won't work out even though everyone will admire you for having the guts to tell the truth instead of just nodding your head and going with whatever happens.

Project management takes a lot of patience and

creativity—without those two things, none of this would be possible. Once everyone works together towards achieving the same objective, you can achieve anything.

Now that you have reached the end of this book, hopefully, you will feel more equipped to take on your own leadership role and be able to help others around you succeed as well.

RECOMMENDED READING

Here is a list of recommended reading. Books I have read and enjoyed for assorted reasons. All are insightful in their own way.

Gladwell, Malcolm. Blink: The Power of Thinking Without Thinking. Little, Brown and Company, 2005. My Book

de Becker, Gavin. The Gift of Fear: And Other Survival Signals that Protect us from Violence. Dell, 1997. My Book

Greene, Robert. The Laws of Human Nature. Penguin Books, 2018. My Book

Greene, Robert. The 48 Laws of Power. Penguin Books, 2000. My Book

Hanson, Jason. Survive Like a Spy: Real CIA Operatives Reveal How They Stay Safe in a Dangerous

World. TarcherPerigee, 2018. My Book

Larkin, Tim. When Violence is the Answer: Learning How to Do What it Takes When Your Life is at Stake. Little, Brown and Company, 2017. My Book

Bishop, Gary John. Unfu*k Yourself: Get Out of Your Head and Into Your Life. HarperOne, 2017. My Book

McKeown, Greg. Essentialism: The Disciplined Pursuit of Less. Crown Business, 2014. My Book

Gladwell, Malcolm. Outliers: The Story of Success. Little, Brown and Company, 2008. My Book

Sinek, Simon. Start with Why: How Great Leaders Inspire Everyone to Take Action. Portfolio, 2011. My Book

Manson, Mark. The Subtle Art of Not Giving a F*ck: A Counterintuitive Approach to Living a Good Life. HarperOne, 2016. My Book

Orwell, George. 1984. Signet Classics, 1961. My Book

Golding, William. Lord of the Flies. Penguin Books, 1959. My Book

Kawasaki, Guy. Enchantment: The Art of Changing Hearts, Minds, and Actions. Portfolio, 2011. My Book

Ariely, Dan. Predictably Irrational, Revised and Expanded Edition: The Hidden Forces That Shape Our Decisions. HarperCollins, 2009. My Book

ABOUT THE AUTHOR

Frank Lazaro is a seasoned executive, accomplished inventor, and technology enthusiast with a passion for driving profitable growth through innovative products and services. With over 20 years of marketing, technology, and strategy experience under his belt, Frank has established himself as a results-driven global executive.

Frank's impressive portfolio of US patents for business processes and product design sets him apart as a true innovator in his field. Throughout his career, he has held key positions at world-renowned brands such as Deloitte, AT&T, and First Data, gaining invaluable experience across multiple industries, sectors, and verticals.

With his natural talent for creating and marketing products that build revenue, Frank has built highly effective teams and programs that have delivered exceptional results. His unwavering dedication to technology and its transformative power has helped him to stay ahead of the curve and innovate in a fast-paced, ever-changing industry.

He is a dynamic leader with a proven track record of delivering results through a combination of innovation, strategic planning, and effective team management. His passion for technology and creating solutions that drive growth is unmatched, making him a valuable asset to any organization.

www.ingramcontent.com/pod-product-compliance
Lightning Source LLC
Chambersburg PA
CBHW070706130626
46553CB00005B/1861